WORDS OF PRAISE FOR
KISSED THE GIRLS AND MADE THEM CRY

"Lisa Bevere is one of the most transparent, direct, and right-on-target women of God I know. That's why you can trust that what she shares in this book has come from a lot of prayer, a life in order, a history of knowing God on an intimate level, and a heart devoted to helping people.

At a time when women are desiring to move into all God has for them, they are being lied to and stolen from by the enemy of their souls. Lisa speaks to that problem with truth and clarity and a writing style that draws the reader in and doesn't let go. I know because once I started the book I couldn't put it down. This is a book that is desperately needed today and is a must-read for every woman, no matter what age. How I wish I'd had access to this kind of information when I was a teenager."

— **Stormie Omartian**
Best-selling author of *The Power of a Praying Wife*

"Lisa has used God's word to shed 'true light' on how God intended things to be, rather than the distorted way they have become. This is a great book for my daughter and yours and anyone who wants to find freedom in God's plans for men and women."

— **Steve Arterburn**
Best-selling author of *Every Man's Battle*, *Avoiding Mr. Wrong*, and *Finding Mr. Right*; and founder of Women of Faith™

"Lisa deals with the heart issues of a woman's sexuality with beauty, grace, and strength. God is calling all women to reclaim their sexual destiny.

I believe Lisa has touched the heart of God and returned the garments of sexual dignity to women. Restoration is the heart of our God and the heart of *Kissed the Girls and Made Them Cry*. She has written gracefully and persuasively the intentions of God's heart for purity in their sexuality. I highly recommend this book to any daughter of God regardless of her age. I highly recommend it as an excellent resource for youth leaders, counselors, and parents who love their daughters as well."

— **Douglas Weiss Ph.D.**
Executive Director, Heart to Heart Counseling Center

"In this eye-opening book, Lisa Bevere dares to answer questions about sex that women are asking, and the vast majority of leaders are dodging. Lisa's boldness and non-compromising stand make this a 'must-read' for parents and youth leaders. Most importantly, this book should be read by every woman who sincerely wants God's wisdom to live pure in a perverse world."

> — **Nancy Alcorn**
> President and founder of Mercy Ministries
> of America

"God has given Lisa Bevere wisdom and knowledge beyond her years, and I am very excited about this book she has written. *Kissed the Girls and Made Them Cry* contains spiritually sound advice that will bless young women and help relieve them of the pressure that society puts on them. The book will also be a useful guide for mothers, youth leaders, and singles pastors."

> — **Betty Robison**
> Cohost, *Life Today*

"My dear friend Lisa has done it again! She touches and teaches the heart of women with this powerful new book."

> — **Sheri Rose Shepherd**
> Speaker and author of *Fit for Excellence* and
> *Life Is Not a Dress Rehearsal*

"Lisa speaks with a knowing compassion and insight to the deepest and most secret desires of a woman's heart, and then directs her to the One True Love who alone can satisfy. She unveils the deception and lies of this world's system, bringing value and dignity back to true femininity."

> — **Katie Luce**
> Cofounder, Teen Mania

"As one who's written often about sexual purity for men, I am constantly asked, 'What about us women? We are struggling with sexual sin, too!' Women need to hear from women on this issue, and Lisa is just the woman to do it. God has literally transformed my life through the Beveres' books many times. Lisa has clearly taken the time to pray, fast, and seek God's heart on this topic, so I'm confident this book will transform your life as well."

> — **Fred Stoeker**
> Coauthor, *Every Man's Battle*, and *Every*
> *Woman's Desire*

KISSED THE GIRLS AND MADE THEM CRY

Workbook

LISA BEVERE

NELSON BOOKS
A Division of Thomas Nelson Publishers
Since 1798

www.thomasnelson.com

Published in Nashville, Tennessee, by Thomas Nelson, Inc.

Some material for this workbook is taken from *Kissed the Girls and Made Them Cry,* © 2002 by Lisa Bevere. Published by Thomas Nelson Publishers.

Unless otherwise noted, Scripture quotations are taken from the HOLY BIBLE, NEW INTERNATIONAL VERSION®. Copyright© 1973, 1978, 1984 by International Bible Society. Used by permission of Zondervan Bible Publishing House. All rights reserved.

Scripture quotations marked "NKJV" are taken from the New King James Version®. Copyright © 1982 by Thomas Nelson, Inc. Used by permission. All rights reserved.

All songs quoted are recorded by Desperation Band on *Desperation: From the Rooftops*/29862. For more information or to purchase product, visit verticalmusic.com or call 1-800-533-6912.

ISBN: 0-7852-6113-3

Printed in the United States of America

7 6 5 4 3 2 1 VG 08 07 06 05 04

Contents

INTRODUCTION

This workbook is my response to daughters from all over the world who've written requesting something to help them draw a bit closer and go a bit deeper. You are the daughters who, regardless of your biological age, have pressed in to embrace God's ageless dream.

You know sexual purity is not a youth issue . . . but a woman issue. This pain has crossed all generations and age brackets. But where there is purity and healing, the blessing extends to all as well.

I send my thanks to every daughter from New Zealand, South Africa, Australia, France, England, Nigeria, Canada, and the U.S.A. who took the time to write. (Some of you have even made your own worksheets.) You have lent your voices as strength and encouragement to the daughters of the Most High.

Dear friends, thank you for letting your hearts break over this nightmare and allowing His Spirit to stir you to action. As you read, may you find yourself equipped and empowered and may your beauty be magnified with His splendor.

—*Lisa*

GETTING THE MOST
OUT OF THIS WORKBOOK

I have an aversion to the whole concept of "work" in workbooks—so why this one?
Well there are just some things we have to "work" through. And sexual purity is one
of them. For example, it is not a youth issue . . . it's a woman issue. Its pain crosses all
age brackets and economics. If we dig deep we'll expose these dark places to His light.
For if disobedience and wounds bring a curse, then surely repentance and renewed
commitment to purity will bring healing and blessing which will extend to all as well.

Because this is for women of all ages, it's designed to be an interactive and intimate
approach to the truths found in *Kissed the Girls and Made Them Cry*. Its goal is to connect you with His living Word so it will become flesh in your life. Please know this is
for individual study as well as a tool for mothers and daughters, small groups, youth
ministry, and women's studies.

KISSED THE GIRLS AND MADE THEM CRY CURRICULUM

We have compiled a complete kit. This includes the DVD/video series, Purity's Power,
a bonus Question and Answer DVD/Video never before available, all recorded with a
live audience at Life Today studios. It also includes the *Kissed the Girls and Made Them
Cry* book and workbook along with leader's suggestions—and to put all these truths to
song, the Desperation Band's *From the Rooftops* CD. To incorporate this life-changing
series in your women's ministry, youth or small group or individual study, check out
the ordering information in the back of this workbook, or visit www.lisabevere.org, or
call us at Messenger International, 1-800-648-1477.

WORKBOOK ELEMENTS

BIG IDEAS

These are condensed quotes or concepts brought forward from the book, *Kissed the Girls and Made Them Cry,* and will be helpful as you work through the units.

HOLY MOMENT

This section provides a place to pause and pull back from all around you and embrace His truth, presence, and love. Holy Moments can happen by meditating on His goodness or just by breathing a prayer. It is time set apart for just you and Him—an intimate glimpse of His love, healing, vision, beauty, splendor, and promises. In the book of Psalms they called this dynamic *Selah*, a time to be still and know.

COLLAGE

God designed us to be inspired by imagery and beauty. Here we will actively cultivate this by gathering inspirational images. As we do this, note your feelings in order to remember "what" and "why" they spoke to you. These pictures will lend sight to what God is doing and give us a visual journal of what will be. They should capture glimpses of dreams and hopes as well as confront and expose our enemy. This is not an activity to be skipped, and feel free to allow it to be a work-in-progress. This is important because daily we're bombarded by images: some beautiful—others destructive. We're going to freeze-frame images which strengthen and inspire.

VOICE OF A DAUGHTER

These are letters from women of all ages who—like you—have found Him faithful. They have chosen to share their insight and hopes, as well as their longing for more. You will hear cries for love, blessing, and a mother.

NOTE TO MOMS

These insights and words of encouragement will help you face off with your own issues and empower you to bless and equip your beautiful daughter.

DREAM MOVIE

Certain movies speak powerful and impacting messages to women of all ages. I'll recommend a few you can watch and discuss with your daughter or share your perceptions with others. Feel free to cuddle up and watch them alone as well; then simply record your reactions and thoughts.

SONG TO MAKE IT REAL

I'll recommend some spirit-breathed music that speaks specifically to the areas of healing and hope we work through in that chapter. These songs have the power to transport you into God's presence. I'll drop in lyrical excerpts of these songs, with ordering information in the back of the workbook.

MAKE IT YOURS

In this section journal your thoughts and personalize His truths, thereby making them your own.

MY PRAYER FOR YOU

These are scattered hopes and longings I have breathed for you in prayer.

Throughout the workbook are questions to be answered. Some will have answers provided at the end of the book. These will be marked with asterisks. But most of these questions are for you. There are no right or wrong answers, just your truth.

This workbook is a message from a generation of mothers and mentors who've known regret, in the hope you might be kept from our failures and inherit the promises and not the pain. It is a tool for mothers who feel hesitant to tell their daughters to say "no" because years ago they themselves said "yes." It is a vehicle for women—young and old—to break free from the horrors of a nightmare and return to His dream of hope, rest, and peace.

One

GOD'S
BEDTIME STORY

Working Our Way Back to the Dream

Read chapter one in *Kissed the Girls and Made Them Cry*, and view session one of *Purity's Power.*

Voice of a Daughter

I am 15 years old and I personally would like to thank you for stepping up and taking this stand on purity. I believe firmly that this nightmare truly does have to be turned back into a dream.

–U.S.A.

1. What is your definition of purity?

Purity is not perfection. It knows its worth and doesn't let anything that's unworthy near it. It's seeing the consequences and knowing if it's worth it.

Why is it important?

Sometimes or most of time judgement is wrong. Ask God for forgiveness and definately you will recieve it. You gain purity from mistakes.

What empowers us to remain pure? (*Kissed the Girls and Made Them Cry*, page 5)

Mistakes that we learn from.

2. Do you feel surrounded by a lot of rules "dos and don'ts" in male-female relationships?

I do but most of time I feel like it's just sexist rules and I don't follow them.

What are some of these?

That a girl should always clean after a guy. A guy leads and girl follow. It's okay for a guy to go out and have fun but not okay for a girl.

What do you think about them?

Most of them I disagree with. But guy lead girl follow I agree. He should always help her guide her way but never telling her what to do. Everything should always go both ways.

Is it hard to follow rules? Why?

Yes because I feel more like we are individuals that decided to put ourselves in this situation. No matter what the outcome is God made us to serve our husbands but they must do the same in return without any expectations.

In my experience rules only truly work when they're applied to games. It would seem our present culture is very busy game playing rather than living life authentically.

3. If rules can not set you free, what can? (*Kissed the Girls*, page 10)

When two people or two individuals find themselves in each other I think that is beautiful. There is no rules needed to love the other person with all your heart. The love that God has blessed them with will guide them and make them free.

4. How do "rules" and "truth" differ?

Rules could be cancelled but truth can't. Truth is something that's happening or something that already happened and can't be changed. Rules can always be broken.

5. What are your thoughts on, "You can go as far with your boyfriend as you are comfortable doing in front of your father" (earthly or heavenly)?

Earthly, because there are things that I will do in front for your boyfriend as in wearing your bathing suit but not your father. And vice versa.

If you're a parent would you want your daughter to embrace this motto?

Yes, but if she doesn't I would like to know.

6. Why do you think fathers are the best at protecting the virtue of their daughters?

She was born as a diamond in his eyes. He has the strength to protect her.

It is not hard to see our culture's sexual climate is both overwhelming and overbearing, but the purpose of this workbook is to draw you back to a place of truth and, therefore, freedom. It is my earnest prayer the dream will overtake your nightmare no matter where it has violated your life.

Voice of a Daughter

I just finished reading your book; it made a big impact on my life! I learned SO much. I prayed the prayers at the end of each chapter with my lips and heart.

–U.S.A.

Now it is your turn—as we work through this together I want you to see my role as a guide. In every question, teaching, movie, or exercise, my desire is to reconnect you with both your Father and Prince.

Have you ever woken from a dream only to be extremely disappointed it wasn't real? Try as you might to reenter it, the dream eludes you. I believe we have these incredibly, amazingly good dreams because one day we will find ourselves in the midst of the most beautiful never-ending one.

Big Idea

Rules cannot combat the nightmare . . . only a dream has this power.

God Promises us:

> *Now we see but a poor reflection as in a mirror; then we shall see face to face. Now I know in part; then I shall know fully, even as I am fully known. And now these three remain: faith, hope and love. But the greatest of these is love. (1 Cor. 13:12–13)*

Think a moment. I'd never thought of a mirror as a "poor reflection" until this Scripture. When I look in the mirror I see myself as I appear. It's my nose, shirt, eyes, and hair looking back. But dig a bit deeper. What you see in the mirror is a captive reflection. It is one dimensional with only the power to reflect. It cannot speak, touch, see, hear, feel, or smell. It only reflects what's presented. And when we turn away . . . it is gone.

But behind this reflection there's a dream. I believe all women dream of beholding an image of breathtaking beauty. This image would prove so captivating it would have the power to set us free from all earthly pain, rejection, and abuse.

Do you know just such an image is your destiny? Right now a mere fraction of this is reflected in our earthly life. But the day is coming when we'll possess the full. We'll leave this realm of part and promise, and embrace our deepest longings and desires. There are three essentials we need to bring us to the other side: faith, hope, and love.

Because this is to strengthen your resolve and heal any breaches in the beauty of your sexuality, it is important you become skillful with these essentials. Let's tackle them in order and lay a foundation. Settle this in your heart . . . the words we study are alive and long to speak to us. Let's pray:

HOLY MOMENT

Father,

I come to you in the name of Jesus empowered by Your Holy Spirit. Illuminate my eyes to see, my ears to hear, my mouth to speak, and my heart to believe. I want to know and be known. I want to heal and be healed. I make your Word the ultimate and final counsel in my life. Release Your dream in and through me. Quicken every dead place and remove all captivity as You empower me with faith, hope, and love in the most holy name of Jesus. Amen.

FAITH

First, faith: Lay aside the pat definitions and let's personalize it. I want you to think of it as a language of the spirit. It is the way God speaks to bring forth life out of death and beauty from ashes. It has the power to release strength when we're weak and courage when we're afraid. It does not say where we are or where we've been but repeatedly declares the beauty of where we're going.

> *And without faith it is impossible to please God, because anyone who comes to him must believe that he exists and that he rewards those who earnestly seek him. (Heb. 11:6)*

God is asking us to simply believe He is and that He is good to those who seek Him with all their hearts. He wants you to release and agree with His blessings and dream of you. Read the following Scripture in light of what we've discussed.

> *Now faith is being sure of what we hope for and certain of what we do not see. (Heb. 11:1)*

Faith is a certainty of something we now only hope for. It is not ours because we've been "good" or because we've done everything right . . . it is ours because of what was done on our behalf on the cross. When we put our faith in Christ and surrender to His Lordship, we receive what His life and death established. In faith we forget what is behind and press toward what is ahead.

> *For we also have had the gospel preached to us, just as they did; but the message they heard was of no value to them, because those who heard did not combine it with faith. (Heb. 4:2)*

Big Idea

Faith has the power to release destiny where there has been destruction. It is essential, for without it you cannot please God.

It is useless to hear promises if you never allow them into your heart. We mix promises with faith when we bravely say "Amen" or "So be it." God loves it when we actively choose to believe.

MAKE IT YOURS

In the space provided tell Him what you believe. You can use the following as a guide:
Begin with something like "You are the one true and living God" . . . then follow with
a declaration of His goodness ("Father, You alone are good and never leave . . ."). Then
personalize His promise (choose any Scripture) write it out in first person, date it, and
finish with an "Amen" or "So be it."

> You are the one true and living God
> that has the power to do and control
> anything that you want. Instead you let
> us be us and learn from our mistakes.
> From all the sins and struggles i've committed
> and been through you will always be there.
> Father, You alone are good and never leave
> my side when i needed you to hear my
> pain, struggles and happiness. Thank you You
> for Your love. In Jesus' Name. Amen.

HOPE

Hope is tied to vision or dreams. It's the image we long to embrace as real, the reflection fully realized.

> *But by faith we eagerly await through the Spirit the righteousness for which we hope. (Gal. 5:5)*

Faith calls for the hope we await. *Faith* sets it in our future and *hope* gives us a reason to dream now.

> *(For the law made nothing perfect), and a better hope is introduced, by which we draw near to God. (Heb. 7:19)*

This "better hope" is life free from rules where love directs the heart and God invites us closer. Here is empowerment. There is no power in rules, no matter how neatly they're packaged.

Hope is the setting of vision and destiny before even considering guidelines.

Big Idea

Rules never set us free, just as fear and control never keep us safe.

> *In his great mercy he has given us new birth into a living hope through the resurrection of Jesus Christ from the dead.* (1 Peter 1:3)

Finally, hope is alive. This means our vision should grow and expand to capture every dream and image of beauty.

LOVE

> *And now these three remain: faith, hope and love. But the greatest of these is love.* (1 Cor. 13:13)

I love the fact God declares love the greatest. It is to intimately know as we are known. It is the greatest because God is love, not faith or hope. He was, is, and always will be Love, and we are promised:

> *Love never fails . . .* (1 Cor. 13:8)

7. What would you do or believe if you knew you could not fail?

I will make every mistake that I possibly can. I will do all the worst things that can be done and most of all if I knew I could not fail I wouldn't try to succeed.

Do you want to hear something awesome . . . all God wants is you! Adventure calls. This path is laid before you stretching as far forward as the end of your days and as far back as your mother's womb. A Prince awaits your metamorphosis and arrival. You've glimpsed Him in your dreams and dimly seen the princess in the mirror, for it calls to you no matter your age or marital status.

Now is the time for restoration. You may feel you're living a nightmare and it's been a long time since there's been a dream. Here's a chance to set aside harsh reality and dream again.

HOLY MOMENT

Write a prayer which reflects all you hope God will accomplish as you walk through this study.

Dear God,

As I walk through this book and flip these pages I just hope to gain more knowledge and understandings on why things are the way they are. Why I am the way I am and it's so easy for me fall in love. I pray that You just help me think things through thoroughly and see it through Your eyes. Love is the greatest gift You have ever given to us and I just hope I know how to use it wisely. There are many games that I've played in the past with Love. Now I think about it and I realize that Love isn't a game. Why do people use it as that and love by rules? Why did I do that? Right now I know that You forbid love to leave us empty handed but I just need Your guidance to lead me there trusting these words as I do in You. It's my fault for not trusting in it with all my heart and that's why I know I get to suffer the consequences but You, God, are always there to part clouds and let the sun shine through. I thank You for that. Just be with me as I take these words back to reality. In Jesus name, Amen.

Note to Moms

Do you notice your daughters are watching for your response? They're not listening for your judgment and denouncement. They long for safety at home no matter what they may say to the contrary. Write down some things you can do to create this dialogue and atmosphere.

_____

_____

_____

_____

_____

_____

Voice of a Mother and Daughter

I showed the first video, "How Far Is Too Far," and God put such a strong response in one 14-year-old's heart she has planned an overnight lock-in to show all the videos inviting her whole school via handouts and word of mouth. I get to play mentor and backup to all this. She is planning games, dinner, breakfast and prayer and quiet time to surround the videos . . . everyone will take home a crown to remind and encourage her.

–U.S.A.

Two
WHERE ARE WE?

The Nightmare Looms Large

_R_ead chapter two in _Kissed the Girls and Made Them Cry._

1. As you step back and look around, what evidence do you see of the nightmare?

   What are the lies it whispers?

   What are the lies it screams?

Which ones have you listened to or find the hardest to resist?

2. In what ways have you compromised or been robbed of the following?

Your dignity? Explain.

Your honor? Explain.

Your mystery? Explain

Voice of a Daughter

I had lost all the stuff you wrote about, had shame, regret, I could relate to everything. My precious Lord and I have worked through this book together and I am a new creation.

−Australia

---

3. In what ways has disobedience compromised your dreams?

4. Has disobedience and rebellion ever truly been a friend or source of power to you?

5. What areas of life did you expect the "man" to meet your needs only to be disappointed?

Big Idea

God is not a man that He should lie.
(Num. 23:19 NKJV)

6. What TV shows encourage the concept that the "man" will meet all your needs?

Note to Moms

If you've experienced disappointment in these areas . . . feel free to look back a moment and share any insight you might have.

Only God is always truthful and only He can meet all our needs. In the Garden, Adam and Eve chose to doubt God and embrace a lie.

7. Returning to the book of Genesis, what were some of the immediate losses of this Garden confrontation?*

After the Fall we find woman stripped of her noble origin and authority. In one moment she exchanged joint and complementary dominion for grasping and manipulation.

Likewise the man was reduced to a position of domination and blame as he laid aside his role as the loving, strong leader. And the struggle that still rages began.

Because we can't make this happen for each other, it has given rise to all sorts of twists and perversions from the original plan.

8. How has this given rise to homosexuality?

> ## Big Idea
>
> *Broken and wounded Adams and Eves turn from God and wrestle with each other. Why? They both long to be restored and whole, but don't know how to make it happen.*

9. Do you understand why a man would believe another man could complete him—or why a woman would believe another woman could complete her?

10. Do you notice that even gay couples are striving to be families?

11. With prevailing disappointment with the way things are, broken men and women are trying to find their completion through and with others of the same sex. But being one with someone of the same sex will never heal. Why?*

12. What is everyone really longing for?

Together the free man, Adam, and his beautiful counterpart, Eve, would have been invincible.

13. What possibility and promise does this speak to us today?

Big Idea

When something is complete, it brings forth life.

14. How does this reflect Christ and the bride?

15. Does disobedience have the same effect today?

> ## *Big Idea*
> *When disobedience drive them from God's presence, they forfeited both authority and power.*

16. Do you see the struggle that added insult to their injury when the enemy sowed the idea that the woman was the "problem" and the man was the answer?

We continue to be frustrated in our search for fulfillment as long as we look in all the wrong places. Men are not your problem, nor are they your answer. This struggle continues between emasculated, angry man and wounded, angry woman with each blaming the other and wanting them to make it right, but neither can . . . only God can restore us to the garden of our dreams.

> ## *Big Idea*
> *The man is not your answer, nor is he the problem.*

The prophesied battle between woman and the serpent still rages. (See Genesis 3:15.) Contrary to popular belief, earthly sons of Adam cannot save us from this serpent . . . it will take a heavenly Prince.

17. Give some social trends that evidence this war between women and the serpent:

18. What is the serpent's goal in his assault against the daughters of God?*

Voice of a Daughter

I was molested at age 4. My life, thoughts, actions, and ways were crazy. I wasn't like my sister or cousins. I knew something had happened even at that very young age. The entire world was different, nothing looked the same. I felt something leave me and I held it in, until age 32.

–U.S.A.

---

19. What happens to the men when women are stripped of their dignity, strength, and honor?*

Big Idea

The serpent's goal has always been the same . . . to strip the daughters of Eve of their dignity, strength, and honor.

20. What does it mean to be the "glory" of something? (See 1 Cor. 11:7.)

21. *Glory* is defined as "magnificence, splendor, beauty, wonder, and brilliance." Does this sound like women are inferior to men?

When a culture no longer honors femininity and virtue as noble, its women are tempted to embrace the lesser power of seduction.

If women never connect with their feminine beauty, honor, and dignity, they become incredibly vulnerable to sexual exploitation.

22. This being true, who is ultimately behind this disconnect?

23. With the realization you're wrestling with a serpent, how should this change your approach to the wrestling match on all levels?*

You cry out for the love of a heavenly Prince. And I have a secret to tell you . . . He longs desperately for you.

24. What is going on in our day that has made us so vulnerable?

We obviously live in a day when lawlessness and iniquity abound. When the lawless rule of self reigns, love dies, and our protection slips away . . . Desires begin to shift and change, and lies seem to transform to truths. (*Kissed the Girls,* page 17) The book of Romans describes this present and accelerating condition in the following verses:

> *Therefore God gave them over in the sinful desires of their hearts to sexual impurity for the degrading of their bodies with one another. They exchanged the truth of God for a lie, and worshiped and served created things rather than the Creator—who is forever praised. Amen. (1:24–25)*

25. In which areas has our culture exchanged the truth for a lie?

26. Where have you made this exchange?

When we reject the knowledge of God, we inherit foolishness and depravity, or a state void of morality. The beauty of holiness and the concept of good are lost, and we tumble in the darkness from bad to worse.

> *Because of this, God gave them over to shameful lusts. Even their women exchanged natural relations for unnatural ones. In the same way the men also abandoned natural relations with women and were inflamed with lust for one another. Men committed indecent acts with other men, and received in themselves the due penalty for their perversion.*
>
> *Furthermore, since they did not think it worthwhile to retain the knowledge of God, he gave them over to a depraved mind, to do what ought not to be done. (Rom. 1:26–28)*

When men are emasculated, they seek the sexual to make themselves feel masculine and powerful again. When men are humiliated they'll do anything to recover their strength.

We left the Garden so we could return. Embrace the following verses as His urgent invitation to return to its safety and beauty.

> *"Come now, let us reason together," says the* LORD. *"Though your sins are like scarlet, they shall be as white as snow; though they are red as crimson, they shall be like wool. If you are willing and obedient, you will eat the best from the land." (Isa. 1:18–19)*

> *"Even now," declares the* LORD, *"return to me with all your heart, with fasting and weeping and mourning." Rend your heart and not your garments. Return to the* LORD *your God, for he is gracious and compassionate, slow to anger and abounding in love, and he relents from sending calamity. (Joel 2:12–13, emphasis added)*

Voice of a Daughter

I see now so clearly that all I wanted and expected from my husband I'll never get— because only God can truly give them.

—U.S.A.

Song to Make It Real
Everyone (Praises)

Praises
To the one who saves us
Through His blood He gave us life
And now we come
Everyone

Great in splendor
Lord of everything
Worthy is Your name
Never-changing
Ever-reigning King
Worthy is Your name
All creation rises up
To declare Your wonders
As people everywhere sing
More than able
Always faithful friend
Worthy is Your name
Bright and burning
You're returning again
Worthy is Your name
All creation rises up
To declare Your wonders
As people everywhere sing

Halle-lujah
Halle-lujah

By Glenn Packiam, from the Desperation Band album *From the Rooftops*
© 2004 Vertical Worship Songs/ASCAP

Three

GO, AND SIN NO MORE

God's Response to the Nightmare

$\mathcal{R}$ead chapter three in *Kissed the Girls and Made Them Cry*, and view session four of *Purity's Power.*

Read John 8:2–11 or its account in chapter 3 of *Kissed the Girls and Made Them Cry*. Place yourself in the crowd. Imagine what it would have been like to be there with Jesus—the sense of tension and the longing for the truth you know He will bring. (*Kissed the Girls*, page 21)

> *Now early in the morning He came again into the temple, and all the people came to Him; and He sat down and taught them.*
>
> *Then the scribes and Pharisees brought to Him a woman caught in adultery. And when they had set her in the midst, they said to Him, "Teacher, this woman was caught in adultery, in the very act.*
>
> *Now Moses, in the law, commanded us that such should be stoned. But what do You say?"* (John 8:2–5 NKJV)

1. Why did the teachers of the law and the Pharisees bring this woman to Jesus? How did they expect Him to answer?

2. Who were the Pharisees really after?*

This they said, testing Him, that they might have something of which to accuse Him. But Jesus stooped down and wrote on the ground with His finger, as though He did not hear. (John 8:6 NKJV)

At first He is not willing to look at her or answer them. He bends down and writes in the dust. The finger of God etches letters not recorded for our knowledge. A woman so shamed and frightened could only imagine His glance as contempt. Perhaps in His memory He is seeing another woman attempting to cover her nakedness in a Garden long ago. (*Kissed the Girls*, page 23.)

Big Idea

Never forget Satan's accusations are his attempt to discredit or undermine God.

So when they continued asking Him, He raised Himself up and said to them, "He who is without sin among you, let him throw a stone at her first."

Then those who heard it, being convicted by their conscience, went out one by one, beginning with the oldest even to the last. And Jesus was left alone, and the woman standing in the midst. (John 8:7–9 NKJV)

3. How did Jesus do more than answer their questions?

4. How did these accusers respond? Why didn't they stone her?

5. Jesus was without sin, yet He refused to throw a stone. Why?

Mercy will always triumph over judgment, but legalists always cry out for death until confronted with their unrighteousness. These Pharisees were experts in the law. The following passages were their scriptural justification for condemning this woman:

> *If a man is found sleeping with another man's wife, both the man who slept with her and the woman must die. You must purge the evil from Israel. (Deut. 22:22)*

And if they were both single and sexually involved . . .

> *If a man happens to meet in a town a virgin pledged to be married and he sleeps with her, you shall take both of them to the gate of that town and stone them to death—the girl because she was in a town and did not scream for help, and the man because he violated another man's wife. You must purge the evil from among you. (Deut. 22:23–24)*

6. Under the Mosaic Law, sexual promiscuity was punishable by death. But wait. There was something very wrong and telling with the woman caught in adultery (John 8). . . what was their omission?

7. Clearly under the law the consequences of sin applied to both. Why was just the woman brought forth . . . where was the man?
What was really happening here?

8. Did the woman break the law and deserve death?*

9. What have you seen recently (in the media or social circles) that might look like this?

How was the woman represented and treated?

How was the man represented and treated?

Even under the law men were to be held equally responsible for their choices. The enemy is always looking for ways to divide men and women and distort this powerful image. Remember, men are not our enemies nor are they our answers.

Since the Garden, he's been ruthless . . . the woman must be stripped of her honor, beauty, and power. Far too often his vicious offensive is launched under the guise of religion.

Big Idea

This encounter is so much more than mercy in action . . . it is the Garden all over again.

10. Review Genesis chapter 3 and consider the following parallels between this encounter and the Garden.

   • The woman looks for power and life from the wrong source.
   • She disobeys a direct command.
   • She is caught and is obviously guilty.
   • The man blames the woman.
   • The woman loses more than she gains.
   • God covers her and promises a hope and future.

11. What does Jesus say to the obviously guilty woman?

When Jesus had raised Himself up and saw no one but the woman, He said to her, "Woman, where are those accusers of yours? Has no one condemned you?"

She said, "No one, Lord."

And Jesus said to her, "Neither do I condemn you; go and sin no more." (John 8:10–11 NKJV)

12. What Scripture lets us know His answer is the same today?*

13. Who has taken our judgment?

Jesus refuses to be deterred from His original purpose . . . He comes to save. In light of this He remains silent until all our accusers are gone.

As the woman stood before Jesus she did not defend her actions or question the absence of her partner. This guilty woman modeled our response when we're caught and obviously guilty.

Rationalizing and making excuses negates our need for mercy, which is the only force that triumphs over judgment. If we do not acknowledge our desperate need for forgiveness, we miss out.

When Jesus spoke again to the people, he said, "I am the light of the world. Whoever follows me will never walk in darkness, but will have the light of life" (John 8:12).

14. What role does His grace play in this?

15. What does it empower us to be free from?

16. What does He set us free to do?

17. What is the lie Satan uses to try and keep us captive? (*Kissed the Girls*, age 30)

Do you remember the lie Eve believed? There's freedom in rebellion. Too often—like Eve—we equate rebellion with freedom, and then we're surprised to find ourselves hurt and trapped.

18. After rebellion, what is the enemy's next tactic?*

Jesus waited until every accusing voice was silent before speaking. He does the same with us—when He speaks it usually is in the form of a question.

I cannot tell you the number of times I have messed up. I've said things I shouldn't have and done things I knew better than to do. I didn't need a crowd to accuse me . . . I had my own chorus of voices. "How could you do that? What were you thinking? You'll never learn! You haven't changed!" The list goes on. Usually I feel so bad I imagine even God in heaven is asking and accusing alongside them. I have disappointed everyone, and they are all wagging their heads.

19. Have you felt this way?

20. What tape plays in your head when you mess up?

Do these words ever truly inspire or bring about change?

How do these sentences and phrases compare with the actual words of Jesus?

Here are the facts:

Fact: You've messed up.

Fact: You'll mess up again.

Fact: People will accuse and judge you.

Fact: You will more than likely accuse and judge yourself.

All of the above statements may be factual and true, but they are not *the* truth. Facts inevitability are overtaken by truth. Jesus promised:

"If you hold to my teaching, you are really my disciples. Then you will know the truth, and the truth will set you free." (John 8:31–32)

The truth:

"I have loved you with an everlasting love; I have drawn you with loving-kindness. I will build you up again and you will be rebuilt, O Virgin Israel. Again you will take up your tambourines and go out to dance with the joyful." (Jer. 31:3–4)

Big Idea

Judgment never moves us to a place of freedom

Look at the process: He loves us, draws us with kindness, then He rebuilds us as virgins. Then He gives us tambourines and says to get out there and dance. Get out of the shadows and make some noise . . . let's get this party started!

It's time to turn from the lies and embrace the truth. You are not condemned; you're forgiven.

21. Where is the place you need His mercy to triumph over your judgment?

22. List the areas of your life where this type of love is needed to push you out of the realm of compromise.

HOLY MOMENT

Pray and ask God to meet you there and to commission you to "Go, and sin no more."

I've found women young and old have a hard time leaving life in the shadows because they labor under the law with its guilt and shame. They believe the lie that bad girls no longer have the right to say "No." Intimacy becomes a forfeited dream, and all they can hope for is groping in the dark.

23. Have you heard these accusations?

Far too often wounded, shamed, promiscuous daughters return to the life they hate because it made them feel temporarily whole, desirable, or powerful, yet each encounter robs a bit more of their soul and sense of self. They compromise in the hope somehow this time it will be different. Their aching loneliness will leave. The lover will stay, and someone will tell them they're loved.

It does not work, yet they keep revisiting these dead places. They have faith, but in the wrong prince and kingdom. They've been seduced and abandoned by the dark prince. With this realization, they feel isolated and judge by religion and lose their hope of the kingdom of light. They live in shadows and call it substance until they are desperate. Often it is a life-and-death crisis that wakens them (abortion, venereal disease, abandonment, and divorce).

> ## Big Idea
> *There is something about women who refuse to be denied . . . they get Jesus' attention! He likes desperate, edgy women.*

> *The LORD is with you when you are with him. If you seek him, he will be found by you.*
> *(2 Chron. 15:2)*

By refusing to cover ourselves again with that which ultimately brings shame, we get what we really need . . . the power!

24. What do you think Jesus meant by "I am the light of life"?

Ask Him now to uncover any and all areas of darkness with the light of His grace.

> *For the grace of God that brings salvation has appeared to all men. It teaches us to say "No" to ungodliness and worldly passions, and to live self-controlled, upright and godly lives in this present age, while we wait for the blessed hope— the glorious appearing of our great God and Savior, Jesus Christ, who gave himself for us to redeem us from all wickedness and to purify for himself a people that are his very own, eager to do what is good. (Titus 2:11–14)*

> ## Big Idea
> We must relentlessly pursue His presence, then remain until He speaks and imparts His power.

25. Plug in *unmerited favor* for the word *grace* in this passage. Does it make sense?

For far too long we have heard grace simply defined as unmerited favor . . . but it is so much more.

> *For sin shall not be your master, because you are not under law, but under grace. (Rom. 6:14)*

Grace empowers us to walk in God's unmerited favor. By embracing truth, we're positioned to ask for His grace (or power) to say "No!" We must be brave enough to believe we can fulfill His command to sin no more.

I invite you as daughters of the Most High God to turn from the lie and embrace His truth: You're not condemned; you're forgiven. You're free to leave behind sin and shame and go, and sin no more.

Voice of a Daughter

I wish I'd had this teaching when I was younger. God is so good and gracious to me and is teaching me each day of His grace.

–U.S.A.

MAKE IT YOURS

Write down any areas you still wrestle with . . . the powerless places of shame and shadow. Acknowledge His words as truth, then give these to Him and receive His empowering grace.

_____

_____

_____

_____

_____

_____

_____

_____

_____

_____

Song to Make It Real

I'll Be OK

I will throw myself down at Your feet
I will live out my life on my knees
You alone I run to
No one helps me like You

I'll be OK when I'm safe in Your arms
And the thoughts of this world fade away
I'll be OK with You
I'll be OK when it's You by my side
And the tears of this life wipe away
I'll be OK with You
I'll be OK

I will lay down my pride for Your grace
I will give anything for one look
One look at Your face
You alone I run to
No one helps me like You

I'll be (2x)
I'll be OK with You
I'll be (2x)
I'll be OK

By Jon Egan, from the Desperation Band album, *From the Rooftops*

© 2004 Vertical Worship Songs/ASCAP

four

AWAKENING LOVE

Developing Passion in a Jaded World

ℛead chapter four in *Kissed the Girls and Made Them Cry.*

1. What are the two types of love poised to awaken in our youth?

   •

   •

2. When romantic love is awakened before its time, what do we risk losing?*

A whole lot of time and emotional energy are spent on people who eventually become little more than strangers. I know this is hard to believe when you are in junior high or high school, but anyone who has traveled a few years beyond this season can attest to its truth.

> ## Big Idea
> *Where there's an awakening . . . there is an opportunity as well.*

3. More often than not you will have some regret if you don't have what in place?*

4. If your priorities are properly ordered, and you purposely choose to awaken a passionate love for God, what will these years be to you?*

5. Why do you believe our culture fights so hard to see only earthly romantic love aroused while neglecting our passion for God?

6. Why is it so important that we make this a conscious choice?

To *not* choose is, of course, to choose. If we do not deliberately choose life, we will find other influences making choices for us. The heart is not easily divided in its affections. The wise Solomon knew and understood this dynamic and with telling foresight penned this charge to the youth:

Remember your Creator in the days of your youth, before the days of trouble come and the years approach when you will say, "I find no pleasure in them." (Eccles. 12:1)

7. Why do you think he said, "Remember"?

8. What does this really mean?

When we think of the word *remember* it no longer carries the weight it used to. We might use it in sentences like, "Remember to turn in your homework." Or "Remember to get the mail." But these are transitory charges for isolated incidents. To "remember" something is a much more weighty aspect. In America we say, "Remember the Alamo!"

9. Our time of youth is described as the season before the days of trouble. What does this mean?*

Big Idea

Remember *is a charge to never forget something of great importance.*

If we understand this time as a unique season of preparation and seek God for His wisdom, things will go well with us. But if we don't, we will squander our time of strength and preparation—we'll look back with regret. It is your time of transition when you stretch your wings, shake off childhood, and step into what is usually the longest season of life . . . adulthood.

Far too often we don't know how to awaken a love for God, or do not seize the opportunity while in our youth, and now attend the school of regret.

We spent time and strength pursuing romantic love and are a bit jaded with the whole "love" fantasy. Others of us were hurt and are now guarded. Some are disappointed and dreamless. Whatever your case . . . it is time for a change. *It is time for love to awaken.*

There is no need to be frightened by this, God understands how scary this can be and has already made provision for our fears.

10. What are the two reasons we should be fearless in receiving His love?*

-

-

He is faithful even when we were faithless. He loved us before we even glanced His way, and this love is forever.

"I have loved you with an everlasting love; I have drawn you with loving-kindness." (Jer. 31:3, emphasis added)

Notice the past-tense terms: "have loved." It was settled long ago, and it's *never* going to change. God reached out and did everything in His power to draw us and capture our attention. He has given His all, and it is settled with Him.

We determine which type of love arises and dictates our actions. Romantic love can rest and dream in this season until its awakening. This affords natural passion a break while we

Big Idea

In our youth love awakens and our heart is directed.

arouse a passion for God. The trick is loving intensely in one area while remaining passive in the other.

11. How is our love for God aroused or awakened?*

Take it to your breast and marvel at the wonder of it. Even though our behavior is often unattractive, He presses near and declares, "I love you."

12. In what ways has God done this in your life?

Big Idea
The first step is to embrace God's love for us.

Perhaps even this book is a declaration of His love for you! Think about it . . . it is not His judgment reaching out to you . . . it is His goodness and kindness!

Or do you show contempt for the riches of his kindness, tolerance and patience, not realizing that God's kindness leads you toward repentance? (Rom. 2:4)

13. This truth presents us with another choice. Upon hearing such a declaration . . . how do we respond?

HOLY MOMENT

Write your response to this irresistible love. Tell Him what this revelation and realization means personally to you.

_____

_____

_____

_____

This happens by moving beyond acknowledging His love and choosing to pursue knowing Him. It is the choice to embrace and respond to what we cannot see, but knowing *how* to walk that path is not always immediately clear.

How do we respond to this Prince we cannot see? There are ways to glimpse Him even now.

For since the creation of the world God's invisible qualities—his eternal power and divine nature—have been clearly seen, being understood from what has been made. (Rom. 1:20)

> ## Big Idea
> *The second step is to respond to His advances.*

14. Look at nature. What do you see? Name some things in nature that lend insight to God's divine character in the following areas:

His beauty

His power

His faithfulness

His majesty

His splendor

His love of diversity

> ## Big Idea
> *Immediate gratification always looks better than treasured hope.*

I'll share mine as well. I glimpse His beauty in flowers, His power in ocean waves, His faithfulness in the sunrise, His majesty in mountains, His splendor in the stars, His love of diversity in each ethnic group. For each of us, these words conjure different images.

If we lay hold of this revelation, then every good and beautiful thing becomes a gift. Allow yourself to take it in and love you with its loveliness. In this we see and touch His invisible qualities or nature. His personality and delight is captured in the details, large and small. Because we're loved, we watch for Him and see things differently.

15. What have you seen today that spoke His love?

Music has the power to arouse desires deep within us. It quickens what was previously dormant. Music has always been a haven for blossoming love, for songs have the power to transport us.

16. What songs moved you when you were a teen?

Big Idea

There is a divine connection between love and music. They expand and reveal each other.

17. What type of songs moved you before you were a teenager?

18. What songs move you now?

Words immersed in music touch places in our hearts nothing else can reach. Lyrics have the power to remain in our minds longer than spoken words. Most of you can recall a song in its entirety after hearing the first few notes.

The influence of music intensifies as we enter adolescence. It speaks for us when words are hard to express, because our feelings are tangled or overwhelming. What songs speak for you now?

19. What is your favorite love song?

Big Idea

Songs lift our truest and deepest emotions closer to the surface and transport us closer to the heart of God.

20. What is your favorite worship song?

21. Comparing the lyrics, is there a correlation? If so, write any parallels:

We're drawn irresistibly to music in the season when love awakens. This awareness comes when we're the most emotionally vulnerable, for music can comfort or enflame.

22. In light of this, how important is the music we listen to?

Music has the power to usher us past our present reality and into the very presence of God.

> *But You are holy,*
> *enthroned in the praises of Israel. (Ps. 22:3 NKJV)*

23. Why should we guard our hearts? (Proverbs 4:23. Pages 47–48 of *Kissed the Girls*)

> ## Big Idea
> *Praises exalt the position, power, and authority of God in our lives.*

24. What determines the direction of our decisions and our affections?

25. Read Psalm 16:1–2, 8–9. What is David doing, and how is he doing it (*Kissed the Girls*, page 48)? How do you "set" your heart? How is your heart transformed?

26. How do you continue your romance with God (Rom. 10:9–11)?*

HOLY MOMENT

Ask God to pour out His love into your heart (Rom. 5:5).
Ask Him to stir your passion for Him.

Note to Moms

How can we encourage our daughters to awaken the right kind of love? One way is to emphasize what is important. Make this connection by sharing some moments and music choices from your teen years. How did music affect you? What would you do differently? Tell her. They love hearing how it used to be!

Voice of a Daughter

I once had a void in my life. When I got saved I still didn't find love and tried almost everything the world had to offer . . . But one day God said, I love you too much for you to continue in sin. Right then I was completely transformed. I have true love now with the Almighty!

–U.S.A.

Song to Make It Real
The Whole Earth

The whole earth is full of Your glory (Echo)
The whole earth is full of Your glory (Echo)

And You reign victorious

You reign victorious over all
For great is the Lord
And worthy of praise
Lift up your voice
And lift up His name
The heavens declare
Our God is the King
We join in the song that the angels sing

The nations will praise You forever (Echo)
The nations will praise You forever (Echo)

For You reign victorious
You reign victorious over all

The whole earth is full of Your glory

By Jared Anderson, from the Desperation Band album *From the Rooftops*
© 2004 Vertical Worship Songs/ASCAP

five

SLEEPING BEAUTY

Awakening the Prince

*R*ead chapter five in *Kissed the Girls and Made Them Cry*, and view session three of *Purity's Power.*

Voice of a Daughter

You spoke of women wanting to be treated like a princess and longing for a prince, of how Jesus truly sees us, and how God our Father truly loves us. As I read these words and listened to the videos, for the first time in a long time, I actually felt hope. I could be loved and I could love properly. I actually began to experience the love of my Father in a way I never had.

–Canada

A dream is a wish your heart makes when it's fast asleep.

–Walt Disney

1. Revisit an amazing, wonderful dream you've had. Describe some key elements or feelings surrounding it: (If you can't remember your dreams, move on.)

I know in a number of my favorite I can fly! More than anything flying speaks of freedom. I escape all that holds me back and rise above all that holds me down. From this vantage point everything is insignificant compared to the exhilaration of my freedom!

2. Looking again at your dream, what do you think these amazing feats or feelings represent?

3. What were the dreams of your childhood?

4. Where are those dreams now?

5. Do you still believe these dreams can come true?

Big Idea

God is the master storyteller. The concepts of Love, Battles, Princes, Princesses, Kingdoms and Happily Ever After, are all His.

6. Look again at the story of Sleeping Beauty on pages 53-56 of *Kissed the Girls and Made Them Cry*. Do you see yourself in the story?

7. Stories express the deepest longing of our hearts. Which fairy tale, movie, or book is your favorite?

8. What Bible personality do you most identify with? (Example: Esther, Ruth, etc.)

9. What is it about this person's story that makes you feel connected?

Big Idea

We want someone who looks deep enough to see beyond our captivity and find beauty.

10. In your own story . . .

    What would you look like?

    How would you act?

How would you be loved?

What would you be loved for?

Chances are this is more real than the "you" projected to others. The sad truth is rather than live authentically most of us are content to live safely.

In actuality every woman longs to be loved for something others have failed to discover—an aspect unique and special to her.

Jesus is definitely willing and able to unearth the hidden treasure and bring life out of death. Who else could have transformed the ultimate symbol of shame and death (a cross) into a symbol of life and beauty? He stands with you as you pass areas of pain, sin, and captivity through the transformation of the cross. Only He can take your nightmares and turn them into dreams.

11. If you've slept too long in a dreamless state, there's an urgent call . . . to awaken now to the Prince. Why?

> ## Big Idea
>
> *Fairy tales speak to the deepest desire of women . . . they might awaken from a passing nightmare to be forever transported to a dream.*

12. What areas in your life remain dreamless or hopeless?

13. Are you willing to allow the Prince to awaken you from the dust and shadows and leave it all behind to embrace His life?

14. What does your room or place of captivity look like? Where were (or are) you trapped? Is it a room you know or just a dark place?

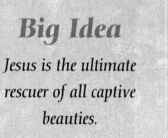

Big Idea

Jesus is the ultimate rescuer of all captive beauties.

15. Who or what imprisoned you there?

16. If there is such a place of pain that remains for you, I want you to capture it now and confront it with the Prince at your side.

HOLY MOMENT

Pause, close your eyes, pray, and invite the Prince into this place, this moment, this incident that violated you. Ask Him to expose the darkness with His glorious light. Let Him wash away your guilt and fears. He is more powerful than the shame and fear . . . ask Him now to rescue you.

17. We discussed the spinning wheels and how Sleeping Beauty's parents made them illegal, hid, and destroyed them rather than instruct her in their proper use. How does this relate to our education and preparation for purity?

18. Why do we see so much fear in this picture?

Like the spinning wheels in *Sleeping Beauty,* our sexuality is not bad or something to be burned and made illegal. It is a good thing. We all understand the problem: When we are careless with good things, they are subjected to abuse or misuse.

Note to Moms

Delayed curses are the most perilous. As time washes over them, they lose some of their immediacy, because delay often breeds complacency or false confidence. Both of these dynamics can make us casual in the face of danger.

When it comes to sexuality, most parents are guided by fear . . . but it is never a wise counselor. Fear deals in rules and extremes rather than in wisdom and moderation. Shame is never a wise guide either, because it keeps you from equipping your sons and daughters.

• *Write some steps you can take to equip your daughter in a healthy empowering way:*

_____
_____
_____

• *What shame issues of your own do you need to bring to His light for healing?*

_____
_____
_____

Other parents feel like hypocrites, so they say nothing. Some have adopted the cultural perspective of sexuality and endeavor to be peers or friends of their children, and therefore they instruct them on how to be responsible by making birth control and sexual experimentation a reality for their children.

Voice of a Daughter

There were some interesting reactions from people who had great relationships with unsaved parents. The video shed so much light about what we should have been taught and why, that some of the girls were really hurt that their parents encouraged them to experiment, live their lives the way they wanted and didn't teach them the truth.

The Holy Ghost brought a lot of stuff to the surface, our suppressed anger and disappointment. We encouraged everyone to go before the Lord, be totally upfront then ask for the grace to release it to Him and forgive their parents (and anyone else who had input) and then to hold on to the truth and let it grow.

—New Zealand

19. How about you? What were you told (out of good intent) that made you think sex was bad? (This could be through books, parents, friends, church groups, etc.)

20. What "bad" advice did you receive that encouraged or gave you permission to experiment with your sexuality? (School, magazines, peers, parents, etc.)

Voice of a Daughter

I can't even remember my mom teaching me the value and importance of "saving myself." Sex was never talked about at home, and was considered rather taboo. So with no boundaries in place, I started "experimenting" from the age of 15 with lads who had little or no respect for me . . .

–England

Think about this Scripture:

Once I was alive apart from law; but when the commandment came, sin sprang to life and I died. I found that the very commandment that was intended to bring life actually brought death. For sin, seizing the opportunity afforded by the commandment, deceived me, and through the commandment put me to death. (Rom. 7:9–11)

21. What are your thoughts on this in light of Sleeping Beauty, the curse, and her parents?

This Scripture makes it clear God is not about law or rules. Notice sin always waits to "seize an opportunity to master us." It lurks in the shadows waiting to pounce even while we're trying to do good! This is why we're admonished to walk as children of light. In the light there is no place for sin to lie in wait. Rules create deception, and deception leads us to death.

Looking again at the rules you were taught, try to rephrase each of them into a guideline that would help you to be skillful with your sexuality.

22. What "beauty" does the Bible encourage us to allow to rest?

23. Read Song of Solomon 2:7. Why are we not to awaken your sexual passion until it is God's timing (marriage)?

> ## *Big Idea*
> *God never said it was bad . . . He said it's not time!*

24. How do you know when it is God awakening love or just your own desire?

25. When will our dreams be realized? (*Kissed the Girls,* page 60)

26. Why would He ever deny the ultimate fulfillment of the dreams He placed within us? Read Psalm 21:2 and Jeremiah 29:11.

27. It is easier to live in the present and gratify our immediate desires. Picture yourself at the altar with the man you'll spend the rest of your life with. What will you give him?

28. How will you have set yourself apart *now* and saved yourself for him *then*?

29. If you have already made mistakes, how can you begin to set your course and create new beginnings?

My brethren, count it all joy when you fall into various trials, knowing that the testing of your faith produces patience. But let patience have its perfect work, that you may be perfect and complete, lacking nothing. (James 1:2–4 NKJV)

Big Idea

The promise of sexual fulfillment requires patience.

30. Do you believe God wants this to be perfect for you? Pause and tell Him so. He loves to hear from you.

HOLY MOMENT

Father,

I believe You are not withholding good and beautiful things from me. You have dreams laid out for me. I want all You have for me. I want Your garden of delight rather than the rumble of regret. I believe You are good and faithful. I believe no matter how many times the enemy repeats his lies! I choose You, for You alone are good and the ultimate romantic!

Married or single, longer periods of anticipation create greater longing and desire in each lover and the greater the desire, the stronger the passion, and the more ultimate the fulfillment.

The most precious things in life come with the dynamic of seeking and waiting, sowing and reaping, and ultimately the wait is worth it.

I know when I was younger I didn't appreciate what I had not worked for. My mother bought me beautiful clothes that I would just toss on the floor or stuff in the closet. It wasn't until I was earning money for clothes and doing my own laundry that I learned to appreciate their value.

31. What things have you gotten too quickly, often to your own detriment?

Our sexuality is the one area of love that is commanded not to be awakened before its time. Rather than saying "It is wrong, it is wrong," we would do better to continually say what God says about this area: "It's not time."

32. What things have you had to wait so long for that the very anticipation of them increased the excitement of the whole experience?

33. Why do we settle for earthly princes who only partly and temporarily fulfill our longings?

34. How will becoming completely fulfilled in an intimate relationship with the ultimate Prince help you in a later relationship with an earthly prince?

35. As a married woman, have you already learned your husband cannot meet all your longings or fulfill all your dreams? Is this some fault of his?

I believe God alone can fulfill the deepest dream in your life.

Collage

Make a collage containing the elements of your dream. This might include pictures or pieces of gowns, houses, jewelry, gardens, furniture, flowers, phrases, anything that fosters beauty and lends image to the dream. When you are done, make a mental note of the elements it does and does not contain.

Voice of a Daughter

After your first video "How Far Is Too Far?" our discussion afterwards was the value of virginity which no one told us was worth fighting for—even those who came from Christian homes were not taught why to wait and the preciousness of virginity, only that we shouldn't go there or we were not told at all.

–New Zealand

Song to Make It Real

Satisfy

All of my shame You erased
You gave me Your beauty in its place
All of my sorrows You exchanged
For a joy that never fades
You are my everything
Everything You are is everything to me

You satisfy me
You satisfy me
With the riches of Your hand
Everything I am is all because of You
You satisfy

All of the things that hold my heart
All of the pleasures of this life
Cannot compare to who You are
And the treasures of Your love
You are my everything
Everything You are is everything to me

You satisfy me
You satisfy me
With the riches of Your hand
Everything I am is all because of You
You satisfy me
You satisfy me
And I lay my life down
My trophies and my crowns
All because of You
You satisfy

By Glenn Packiam, from the Desperation Band album *From the Rooftops*

© 2004 Vertical Worship Songs/ASCAP

Six

THE ORIGINAL CINDERELLA

Putting on the Slipper

*R*ead chapter six in *Kissed the Girls and Made Them Cry.*

Voice of a Daughter

I want what you described more than anything, so much it makes my heart ache and I feel as if I want to cry. I want to be a princess, I want to be a lady. I'm tired of feeling dirty and bad . . . I've decided that if Jesus says I can have that, then I will wait as long as it takes for Him to bring me the right guy.

–Canada

1. According to Ezekiel 34:16 and Luke 19:10, who is actively and deliberately pursued by our Prince?

2. How does this differ vastly from what we know?

3. Is the selection process of our culture exclusive or inclusive?

4. Have you ever feared you wouldn't make the cut?

5. Why does He do this? Why would He want the lost, hurt, hopeless, and helpless? Why is our Prince attracted to the unattractive?

Big Idea

Our Prince does not pursue the noble daughters of this world . . . He looks for those overlooked by others.

6. Review Ezekiel 16:4–14.

7. Write down any parallels between this abandoned daughter and the present lack of maternal nurturing in our modern culture.

8. How does abandonment differ from abortion?

9. Would it be harder for you to actually hold your child then reject it?

10. Who nurtures those rejected at birth?

Perhaps you were not cruelly abandoned at birth but have the pain of abandonment or intense rejection in another area. If so, describe this place of pain.

11. Do you think the Prince is capable of finding you in this place of neglect?

12. Is He willing to rescue you as well?

13. How does the Prince respond to this infant's fading cry?

14. How does He care for her as she grows?

15. How did He respond to her when it was her time for love? Who is the Prince, and who is the baby?

16. Can you relate to this story on any level? If so give specifics.

He has the power to dispel all death and shadow in your life. He just awaits your response . . . your permission to let Him love you. He wants your life and freely gave His in exchange. All He asks in return is the love of a bride.

Big Idea

Never doubt this . . . God's response to every curse and word of death spoken over your life is "Live!"

HOLY MOMENT

Pause and make it happen now, give Him your pledge of love. He is not asking you to minister for Him or to sacrifice. He is just asking for your broken heart. Breathe a prayer and offer Him your imperfect love. Dearest Lord, I don't even know what the love of a bride might look like . . . but I am willing to learn. Holy Spirit, anoint my eyes to glimpse the bride within me. Begin to adorn me with heaven's love while yet on earth. Wrap me in splendor. *Pause and drink it in.*

17. Define splendor. (*Kissed the Girls,* pages 68–69)

18. Is splendor something you can buy or develop?

19. Do you believe the King of heaven can magnify your beauty with His splendor?

20. Would you believe the King if He called you altogether lovely? What areas fight against this declaration of loveliness?

Why is this true?

Why is it often hard to accept the love of others even though we so desperately want it? I believe it is because each of us carries a long list of our flaws and faults. But God isn't interested in our lists. He doesn't see us as we are now . . . He sees us perfected by His love and freed from all fear. Even now the transformation of His love is making us over. He sees us eternally radiant, the precise reflection of His tender and passionate love. He sees the heart, not the flaps of our skin temporally nipped or tucked by a scalpel.

> ## Big Idea
> *No one can be loved by the King and keep it a secret.*

21. Do you think this is true?

22. Do you think only young women want to be beautiful?

23. In our pursuit of beauty, do you think God has a problem with any of the following?

   • Jewelry?

   • Beautiful clothing?

   • Makeup?

> **Big Idea**
> *Every woman longs to be perfect and perfectly loved.*

   • Plastic surgery?

• What about eating healthy and exercising?

I don't believe He has a problem with any of these things. So what is the real issue here? Trust. God is always bigger than a *thing issue*. He searches the heart and weighs the motives that drive and direct our decisions and source of confidence. He alone knows what we trust in.

> *"But you trusted in your beauty and used your fame to become a prostitute. You lavished your favors on anyone who passed by and your beauty became his." (Ezek. 16:15)*

Beauty is never to be an end in itself. Let's review the way this daughter turned from God. (*Kissed the Girls*, page 69–70)

   a. Trusting in beauty.

   b. Using God-given honor, beauty, or fame to seduce others.

   c. Foolishly giving away the costly to those who don't even truly care.

   d. Turning from His love to seek affirmation from this faithless, passing world.

24. In what ways might you relate to this passage?

Big Idea

We get our life from what we trust in.

25. What does it mean to trust in our beauty? What happens when we trust in beauty? (*Kissed the Girls*, page 70)

This means our self-worth will be vulnerable and threatened by those around us. Do we really want to give them this kind of power over us? Will we ever be good or beautiful enough for them to tell us we are whole?

Ezekiel 16 speaks differently to each of us, yet on some level its story is our own. We were without hope and dying even as our life began. The Prince heard our cry of pain, suffering, and sin. When we are helpless and hopeless, dying in the mire of rejection and the bloodshed of sin, He lifts us. Then moved by love He reverses the curse and cleanses us . . . intimately and completely. After removing the sin and filth of our past He provides for and tenderly nurtures us. Will we blossom in His love? Choosing to reach out when He seems far away, a distant dream waiting to come true?

HOLY MOMENT

In what way have you felt abandoned, with the word "die" written on your forehead? Have you longed to be rescued from the mess and mire of your life? Have you longed to be taken care of and cherished? Have you longed to be loved purely and tenderly by the One who is patient? In what ways have you turned away?

It is so tempting to turn aside to others because we wanted to be touched here and now. We exchange His garments of splendor for gaudy ones and gather flashy trinkets forgetting the promise of glorious jewels. Too often the deceitfulness of present riches and the lust of other things distort the promises of the Prince. So some of us have undressed in the presence of men with whom we had no covenant, hoping their bodies would make us whole, but their hands dirtied again the very places the Prince had so carefully cleansed. (Excerpt from *Kissed the Girls,* page 71)

Big Idea

If we trust in our beauty, we constantly need affirmation. Others become the mirrors and measure of our value and worth.

Even in the story of Cinderella, her beauty was only temporary, an illusion fading at the stroke of midnight. How many of us feel this way? We come home from an evening out, and our mirror reflects a slightly disheveled, shoeless version of what left earlier at the height of glamour. We exceeded our curfew and found ourselves stripped of the magic.

It is noteworthy that when Cinderella's earthly prince found her, she was not radiant. She was again a servant in a cruel household. She glimpsed a dream and was immediately put back into her place by those around her. I am sure she thought, *Who was I kidding? I could never truly be loved or a princess. I looked and acted like one for a fleeting moment, but reality has come crashing down all around me! I am an imposter. Who am I to dream? If the prince knew who I really was, he'd seek another.* But without her knowledge the prince was searching her out . . . glass slipper in hand. She was the only one he wanted.

With our Prince this truth is even more profound. He was never captivated by some projected image of perfection and goodness at the unreal setting of a ball. He sees us at our worst and embraces us. He finds us in filth and washes us. He lifts us when we are weak with nowhere to run and strengthens us.

Voice of a Daughter

I was feeling alone and untouchable. I turned on the TV and Lisa was talking about Kissed the Girls and Made Them Cry. *I could hear the Father talking to me and ordered the book the next day. The Father has spoken so very much to me.*

–USA

God places this dream and longing in each and every woman's heart. Do you honestly know anyone young or old who would want nothing to do with this dream?

I seriously doubt it. If she denies it . . . she speaks out of disappointment. She's silenced her heart and learned to live dreamless.

Song to Make It Real
Beauty of the Lord

Jesus Your love
Has come one step closer
I will trust
That You will never let me go

Jesus Your love
Has won me over
All my trust
Has found no other

I will declare the beauty of the Lord
Nothing compares to the beauty of the Lord
Jesus Your love takes my breath away
Now I'm living every day for the beauty of the Lord

Jesus Your love it takes my breath away
Jesus Your love it takes my breath away
Jesus Your love it takes my breath away
Jesus Your love it takes my breath away

By Jared Anderson, from the Desperation Band album *From the Rooftops*

© 2004 Vertical Worship Songs/ASCAP

Voice of a Daughter

. . . through your encouragement, I have been letting Him hold, caress, and purely love me . . . even though I felt unlovable.

–USA

And now for a visual banquet of another Cinderella:

Dream Movie

It's time to watch a movie. It's quite possibly my favorite. John watched it on a transatlantic flight and then rented it for me, and I loved it so much I bought it years ago for Valentines Day. It is the movie Ever After. I want you to watch it, I mean really watch and then record your feelings in the journal section at the end of this chapter. If you're a mother, cuddle up and watch it with your daughter. If you are a teen, grab some friends and have them over. Even if you have seen it before, I want you to approach it as if it were the first time. Enjoy and record what scenes and phrases speak to you and why.

MAKE IT YOURS

Journal your thoughts:

_____

_____

_____

_____

_____

_____

_____

_____

_____

_____

_____

_____

_____

_____

_____

_____

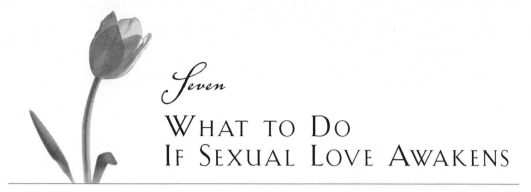

Seven

WHAT TO DO
IF SEXUAL LOVE AWAKENS

Rocking the Baby Back to Sleep

*R*ead chapter seven in *Kissed the Girls and Made Them Cry*.

Voice of a Daughter

I was 23 when I was awakened, not through intercourse, but through touching. At the time, I didn't even know what was happening to me! I was never told ANYTHING about where guys can touch and what you may experience, but after that, I didn't know how to say NO!

–South Africa

1. Why is it easier to awaken love than to get it back to sleep?

2. What is the most disturbing to your sexual rest or sleep?

3. Have you ever felt betrayed by your body's reaction to the various stimuli around you?

4. What was it that aroused or disturbed you?

5. Why is this so hard to escape?

Note to Moms

Reconnect by putting your daughter to bed. It's a great way to address the issues of each day in a private setting. You may be thinking, I just want to get her to bed so I can get a moment to myself! But listen and see what you might hear. More than likely you won't have a deep and meaningful conversation every night, but the comfort of this routine remains, and when she's ready or a need arises she'll speak. Rub or scratch her back while you help her unravel the day. You never want to miss the chance to pray and bless her before she closes her eyes.

Desire is not bad, but it was never meant to be our master.

I know beyond a shadow of a doubt I've developed some of my own intense and quirky cravings. In the book I used the example of my dark, rich, and slightly bitter chocolate preference. But I don't remember being picky when I was younger . . . I'm the one indulging my preference.

6. Think about some preferences, appetites, or cravings you've developed:

- First list some good, harmless, and possibly even beneficial ones:

> ## Big Idea
> *Our desires were never meant to be awakened and then neglected.*

- Now list some others that have been detrimental:

Abuse is best defined as the wrong or inappropriate use of something. Abuse or misuse has the power to turn "good" into something destructive. Sexual addictions are a prime example of this.

There is grave danger in elevating desires or appetites to a place of supremacy. We know this is the case when our desires or appetites no longer serve us but become our masters.

In the context of sex and food, a healthy appetite is important. A healthy appetite is necessary and vital to life and propagation.

> ## Big Idea
> *Indulging the wrong appetites inevitably leads to abuse.*

7. Are there any appetites in your life that started out good and healthy and ended up haywire? If so, what are they? (This could range from shopping to watching TV.)

"Everything is permissible for me"—but not everything is beneficial. "Everything is permissible for me"—but I will not be mastered by anything. (1 Cor. 6:12)

God alone is worthy of mastery. He never abuses this position. We decrease appetite or desire's importance by assigning God preeminence over them. We first put them before the cross, then we curb or control their influence by limiting their intake.

8. Do you remember being rocked to sleep? What feelings did it inspire?

Big Idea

We have the power to develop our appetites and desires, therefore we can increase or diminish their influence as well.

HOLY MOMENT

Write a prayer to your heavenly Father and ask Him specifically to comfort and calm any raw or frightened areas.

_____

_____

_____

_____

_____

_____

"The LORD *your God is with you, he is mighty to save. He will take great delight in you, he will quiet you with His love, he will rejoice over you with singing." (Zeph. 3:17)*

9. Looking closely at Zephaniah 3:17, there are five main points. What are they?

-

-

-

-

-

10. What has the power to save you?

11. What has the power to quiet you?

12. What has the power to surround you with joy?

13. How does joy differ from happiness?

14. If your greatest fear is loneliness, how does Zephaniah answer this?

15. If your greatest fear is powerlessness or vulnerability, how does Zephaniah deal with this?

Voice of a Daughter

The part that ministered to me the most is while you were ministering you told a young girl that while she sang and worshiped God, He would sing a lullaby over her that would put those things back to sleep. That right there set me free. I felt the Lord speaking this to me. I have not had to struggle with those images and desires like I usually do. It is only something the Spirit of God could do!

–U.S.A.

16. If rejection is an issue or fear of yours, how does Zephaniah 3:17 resolve it?

17. If your enemy is depression, how does Zephaniah change this dynamic?

We activate and respond to this type of love, acceptance, deliverance, and power by praising Him. If we want Him to sing over us . . . we sing! And if we want Him to dance . . . we dance!

> *I will praise you as long as I live,*
> *and in your name I will lift up my hands.*
> *My soul will be satisfied as with the richest of foods;*
> *with singing lips my mouth will praise you.*
> *On my bed I remember you;*
> *I think of you through the watches of the night.*
> *Because you are my help,*
> *I sing in the shadow of your wings.*
> *My soul clings to you;*
> *your right hand upholds me. (Ps. 63:4–8)*

The psalm begins with "I will praise you as long as I live." That's a very strong heart determination and one God will not ignore. God cannot resist those who set themselves in pursuit of Him regardless of what disappointments may come their way. When this issue is settled before Him . . . we have His attention. We captivate His heart with just one glance!

A HOLY MOMENT

Say it now . . . tell Him what you will do not only now but for the rest of your life. This doesn't mean you won't mess up, as any married woman can tell you, but it does mean you are striking a covenant. Breathe a prayer now.

MAKE IT YOURS

Write what you saw in the spirit: the abandon, the joy, the commitment. Write your vision now:

_____

_____

_____

_____

_____

As discussed, music is a heart language with the power to bypass our heads and transport us somewhat from our present reality. As we praise Him, the veil is rent and we enter into the dimension of the spirit where we cannot help but lose ourselves and feast on His faithfulness as our soul clings to Him and His right hand upholds us. It is here that the joy of the Lord becomes our strength.

18. Have you ever experienced this amazing dynamic?

If not, know it is available to everyone. For me this level of intimacy rarely happens at church. I have found its enveloping warmth and beauty while at home, alone where I dance with and for Him.

HOLY MOMENT

Right now commit to make this a priority for you. Choose to seek Him until you are found by Him. It is all about the power . . . you need His strength and anointing as you face off with your flesh and battle the formidable foe . . . lust. Find a private room, crank the music, and dance before Him.

Note to Moms

Like Esther I am crying out for the daughters of this generation that they might be spared the destruction of the enemy of their souls who seeks to sell them to death. You can do the same. It is a time as women to lay down our lives to preserve the loves of many daughters yet unknown to us.

In Psalm 35 verse 13, King David shared how he humbled himself with fasting. When we humble ourselves, God is exalted in and over our situation. God outlines the purpose of the fast:

> *"Is not this the kind of fasting I have chosen: to loose the chains of injustice and untie the cords of the yoke, to set the oppressed free and break every yoke?"* (Isa. 58:6)

Fasting breaks chains of injustice, unties the cords of the yoke, frees the oppressed and breaks *every* yoke. Not just the easy ones, but every one! Can we dare to believe this promise? If you do you will choose to fast!

Fasting modifies or changes appetites, so let's now look at how God recommends dealing with the issue of appetites that drive us:

*Put a knife to your throat if you are a man
given to appetite. (Prov. 23:2 NKJV)*

To be *given to* is best described as "mastered
or driven by." Instead of *appetite,* another version uses the word *gluttony.* It describes someone compelled by their flesh rather than led by
the Spirit. This is often played down, but it is
very serious issue. Here are more.

> *Flee from sexual immorality. All other sins a man
> commits are outside his body, but he who sins sex-
> ually sins against his own body. (1 Cor. 6:18)*

And again,

> *Flee the evil desires of youth, and pursue righteousness, faith, love and peace, along with those
> who call on the Lord out of a pure heart. (2 Tim. 2:22)*

19. What does *flee* mean?*

20. What visual image does this paint for you? Give some key words.

> ## Big Idea
> There's only one way to
> dismantle a desire,
> craving, or appetite . . .
> starve it, and you render
> it powerless.

There is nothing casual about this word. In order to flee you must fast! In the following space list any areas the Holy Spirit is asking you to flee. (This could include relationships, music choices, TV sitcoms, movies, jokes, books, etc.)

_____

_____

_____

_____

_____

_____

Looking at the list, these are areas where you might need to fast to get them back into the correct perspective or balance. If secular music is an issue, for example, you could cut it totally out for a month.

It is important to note there is a long-term benefit to fasting something for a season. We recover our perspective or sensitivity, and when the fast is over, we will find ourselves with an increased level of awareness.

For example, I periodically fast TV, and often when I turn it on again I am shocked and grieved by what I experience. I am again sensitive to worldly or unwholesome programs (or commercials). Once this sensitivity is recovered, I don't want to lose it again, so I frequently turn off the TV!

Voice of a Daughter

As I read about fasting, I just knew I had to do that . . . I did my first-ever fast this past weekend. It was amazing! You have cleared up a few issues for me and made some of my own views a lot stronger. I believe the Lord is preparing me for marriage, and your book was another step in the process.

–U.S.A.

Another way to fast is to remove all offending material from our homes. This might include videos, books, or magazines which arouse the wrong desires. (Pornography is never good, even if you are married and it is represented as instructional.)

Heavenly Father,
Quicken by your precious Holy Spirit my awareness of any offending materials in my
home. I want them removed and my home swept clean so your presence can inhabit
every place. (Be still, listen, then follow His leading.)

Voice of a Daughter

The thought of sex and getting that close to someone actually scares me (despite the
fact there are days when I crave it). My prayer is that the Holy Spirit will sing it to
sleep in me until He knows when it's time for it to be awake. I honestly can't even
begin to express what the videos showed me, but I know it was something I've been
looking for, for a long time.

–Canada

MAKE IT YOURS

Use this space to journal and record your fasting experience.

_____

_____

_____

_____

_____

_____

_____

_____

_____

_____

_____

_____

_____

_____

Song to Make It Real
Amazed

You dance over me
While I am unaware
You sing all around
But I never hear the sound

Lord I'm amazed by You
(3X)
How You love me

How wide
How deep
How great
Is Your love for me

How wide
O how wide Lord
How deep
O how deep Lord
How great
O how great is Your love for me

Lord I'm amazed
Amazed by You
Lord I'm amazed
Amazed by You
And Lord I'm amazed
Amazed by You
How You love me

By Jared Anderson, from the Desperation Band album *From the Rooftops*

© 2004 Vertical Worship Songs/ASCAP

Eight

HONORING YOUR FATHER

Receiving a Spirit of Adoption

*R*ead chapter eight in *Kissed the Girls and Made Them Cry.*

Voice of a Daughter

In your video series we loved what you said about "morning love," it made us realize what we wanted so desperately from our parents. I think what hurt so much was realizing the way things should have been in God's plan, and the stark contrast of what we actually had. More and more we understand what the family really is about. Saying that, we have such a resolve to not settle for anything less than our Father's best.

–New Zealand

Voice of a Father

Lisa, thank you from a father's heart for your insight and openness, I believe this could be one of the most powerful books our young ladies have access to. God used your words to speak to me about my role as a father to my two daughters (ages 6 and 7) as well as my role as a spiritual father to the young ladies in my youth group.

–U.S.A.

This is an awesome God dynamic, the hunger of a daughter for her father's best and the heart of a father to love and protect his daughters. But what if there's a major disconnect between fathers and daughters? Could they ever really grasp "the Father's best"? Or would they resign themselves to something less? Even worse, would they mistake abuse for love? How can we recapture the vision of a father's love, wisdom, and protection?

Father . . . the word can produce an incredible range of emotions. For some, he's the one who was always there bringing correction, love, direction, and provision—a strong, sure tower ever ready to protect. For others he's a strict, stern disciplinarian, the one we're afraid to disappoint . . . for fear of rejection.

1. When you think of an ideal father, what images or words come to mind?

2. Is this the role your father played?

3. What role would you like your father to have in this season of life (counselor, protector, provider, coach, etc.)? This will vary according to your age and marital status.

4. Was there a time or situation when you wish you would have listened to your father's advice but didn't? Explain.

5. How might things have been different?

The image of a father is under attack and in question right now as the whole appearance and definition of marriage and family is morphing into something almost unrecognizable. But when our very model for prayer begins with "Our Father in heaven, hallowed be your name" (Matt. 6:9), it's an important dynamic to get our hands and hearts around. How can we possibly relate to a heavenly Father if we're disconnected from our earthly one? The word *hallowed* assigns honor to our heavenly Father, but what does it mean to honor our earthly fathers here and now? *Honor* implies to weigh as heavy or assign an importance to an individual or their word.

This is an incredibly big issue for the women of this generation because the lines have become so blurred. There is no escaping the fact that our relationship with our earthly father will to some degree direct and affect how we relate to God the Father.

When you come before God, do you see evidence of this blurring in your life? Let's go deeper.

HOLY MOMENT

Ask the Lord to reveal the image you hold of Him and how this affects your relationship with Him. Record your thoughts. Tell Him you need to embrace Him as Father and open up the places in your life to Him now. Be specific with areas where you need and want His protection. These will be places where virtue and honor are on the line. Gather the wisdom you need from your Father and write down any specific promises and Scriptures.

_____

_____

_____

_____

_____

_____

I believe fathers are equipped to act as the protectors or guardians of their daughters' virtue, and this can happen even if they are not Christians. But what if you have no father to do this, or even worse—one who violated your virtue?

Note to Moms and Dads

As parents we've all failed in the past, but this would never mean we're not empowered to protect our children's futures. It is not too late to start. When we feel inadequate, we must cry out for God's wisdom and counsel.

If you have no healthy father figure in a human sense, you still have a heavenly One. If you were utterly abandoned or rejected by your earthly father, then you are in position to be utterly and completely adopted by your heavenly One.

And there are some things you need to know about Him:

- He'd never want to see you violated.

- He'd want you protected and nourished.

- He will provide for you.

- He never leaves.

In any given situation you could rightly ask, "How would My heavenly Father want me treated? Would He allow this?"

From this you would have the assurance you should never compromise yourself for fear of loneliness or lack of finances.

If you are certain He would not want you treated this way, be just as certain He'll back you as you take your stand. Don't imagine He'd make comments like "You asked for it by being here" . . . He would not! He would say, "Get out, get home, and be safe! Run to Me and I'll take care of you!"

If you're involved with someone controlling, and you find it hard to stand up to him face-to-face, refuse to meet with him. Better yet, ask your father to handle it for you! (Healthy earthly ones make great bodyguards and defenders!)

> ## Big Idea
> *Fathers are the protectors of virtue for their daughters.*

If you are in an unhealthy, controlling relationship, you need to take back your power!

Abusive, controlling guys only respect someone or something bigger than themselves. And believe me, like all abusers, they're cowards. You do not owe abusive cowards explanations. If you decide it is over . . . it is over.

Our heavenly Father wants to fight these battles for you as well. He will cover and protect you from harm . . . let Him.

This means *submitting* to His counsel. I know this "s" word can be frightening. When we've been burned by one authority, we tend to flinch at all of them. But we can't throw this baby out with the bathwater, so let's define authority. It's not someone who runs around saying, "I am the boss! I am in charge here!" Authority is so much more than bossing others around. It is God ordained for granting protection, provision, direction, instruction, and blessing.

God said in Genesis He chose Abraham to be the father of faith and blessing because He knew he would instruct his children in the things of God. Our heavenly Father's interest is not limited to individuals. He is after the family as well. He wants a legacy of love and covenant, a household of faith with many children!

A generation of fathers needs to be heartbroken and outraged by the merchandizing, marketing, and violation of their daughters. Why? Our heavenly Father grieves over it.

Part of honoring our Father is choosing to walk in godliness. We must consciously choose to spurn the counsel of our culture, humble ourselves, and acknowledge His ways as higher than our own. In contrast with God's truth, the advice we find in magazines and from the gurus of today is mere foolishness.

Girls who enjoy a healthy vibrant relationship with their fathers are much less vulnerable to abusive men. Because they have enjoyed a healthy role model in their home, they recognize the unhealthy when they see it. Daddies who treat their daughters as though they were royal daughters of the King are much less likely to allow anyone to treat them as anything less.

Fathers who compliment and affirm their daughters protect them from looking for other men to do this for them. Fathers who remember what they or their friends were like when they were teenagers are much less likely to allow their daughters to be put

> ## Big Idea
> *Though rebellion appears empowering, it offers no real protection!*

in positions where they can be compromised. Fathers who openly train and instruct their daughters in the matters of male and female relationships are equipping their daughters with the knowledge they need to make good decisions in tempting places.

6. Look back at when you dated the "wrong guy." What was your family dynamic at the time?

Here is our challenge: if we've been abandoned or neglected by authority figures, will we still choose submission to God-given authority (such as youth pastors, parents, pastors, employers, etc.)?

What might happen if you told your father how much you really need him? What if you admitted you really didn't know it all after all . . . what would happen? Ask for his strength because you are under a barrage of mixed messages and need his help to sort it all out. Why not pour it out in a note? Or if you're comfortable, climb in his lap and tell him.

A lot of the messages sent by our culture (such as in TV sitcoms) imply fathers are rather unnecessary (except financially) and often stupid.

7. What voices have you heard that communicate this?

I believe there is a desperate need for men the world over to rise up and protect their wives and daughters and in the process bring healing to the places they've left vulnerable. But this will only happen if we foster this.

I believe the more our culture has stripped men of this role, the more aggressive they've become (abusive, promiscuous, and negligent).

Big Idea
Women should be protected, not violated, by the men in their lives.

8. What might happen if we all determined to honor our fathers? Think of some ways you can do this.

When Dinah was raped by the prince of the land (Gen. 34:2–31), her brothers avenged her by killing the prince and every man of the city. I would say they took their sister's honor seriously. When Jacob questioned them on why they'd been so harsh, they answered, "Should he have treated our sister like a prostitute?" (Gen. 34:31). Now I am definitely not advocating the death sentence for sex offenders, but I am suggesting we've slipped way too far to the left.

Why was Jacob silent . . . could it be he'd been disobedient to God and at some level ultimately put his family at risk?

God had told him to travel to one place, but it was easier (at first) to set up camp in another because he was afraid of his brother.

> **Big Idea**
>
> *We must connect in a healthy, vibrant manner with our father (heavenly or earthly) before we can truly entrust our love to another.*

If this has not happened for you . . . it can. I found myself feeling at a loss in just this way. I cried out, "Father I feel fatherless" and wept overcome with self-pity and pain. But, in the stillness I heard the Father of heaven whisper, "What you see as rejection I see as adoption. When you are totally abandoned by your earthly father you are in position to be completely adopted by your heavenly One." Right then it was settled. I received His Spirit of adoption and began to call Him my Father. It changed everything. It changed the way I loved my husband, the way I loved my children, the way I looked at my future.

HOLY MOMENT

Heavenly Father,

I need to connect if I am to be free to love. I release all my disappointment and rejection to You. I receive the Spirit of adoption promised in Romans 8:15, I receive the Spirit of adoption by whom we cry out, "Abba, Father" (NKJV). I cry out to You now . . . Abba, Father I am Yours and You are mine. No longer will I walk the paths of rejection and disappointment, for You are with me.

In truth it is the father who has the power to bless or hurt his family more than anyone else. The way a daughter allows herself to be treated by her husband is modeled by her father. This relationship determines how she will respond as well. Now you are in position to be fearless in love. Give all to Him.

Voice of a Daughter

I'm 14 years old and my parents bought me the Kissed the Girls and Made Them Cry *book recently. It touched me deeply, and opened my eyes to many things I had been doing wrong.*

–U.S.A.

Dream Movie

What a Girl Wants

As you view this movie, think about some of the following:
What was the young woman's favorite story?
Why was she saddened by the wedding dance when she was not yet in a position to be married?

MAKE IT YOURS
AND REACTION TO THE MOVIE

Journal your thoughts here:

_____

_____

_____

_____

_____

_____

_____

_____

_____

_____

_____

_____

_____

_____

_____

_____

_____

_____

_____

_____

_____

_____

_____

_____

_____

_____

_____

_____

_____

_____

_____

_____

_____

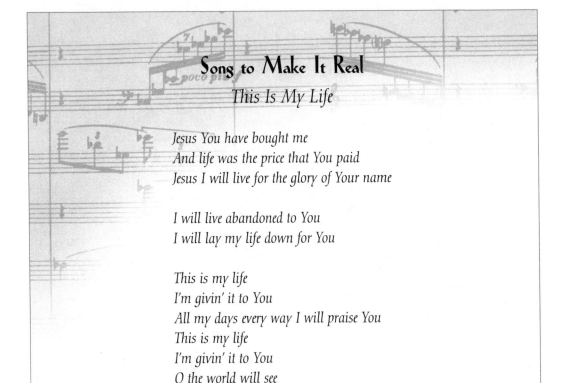

Song to Make It Real
This Is My Life

Jesus You have bought me
And life was the price that You paid
Jesus I will live for the glory of Your name

I will live abandoned to You
I will lay my life down for You

This is my life
I'm givin' it to You
All my days every way I will praise You
This is my life
I'm givin' it to You
O the world will see
This is my life

By Jon Egan, from the Desperation Band album *From the Rooftops*

© 2004 Vertical Worship Songs/ASCAP

Nine

LIVING SACRIFICES

The Power of the Cross

*R*ead chapter nine in *Kissed the Girls and Made Them Cry.*

Voice of a Daughter

God has challenged me through your book to set a high standard of purity in my relationships. I know it'll continue to be a daily crucifying of my flesh and God will give me the strength. Though I've been a Christian for 3 years, I'd never really yielded my body to Christ. Now I do. Thank you!

–Singapore

Why should we confront our old issues? Why not just let them lie until they become an issue? Because . . . areas you do not confront will not change.

The Roman Empire was successful as long as it was offensive in its expansion, but it ran into problems when it moved into the defensive stance of protecting its borders. We need to boldly confront lies and not wait until they set up camp around our borders.

You cannot afford to be casual with this. These areas will not remain silent forever. All

Big Idea

Know without a doubt . . . if you embrace it, the cross has the power to change your paradigm on everything.

things must eventually be brought to the cross for a confrontation. This means different things to each of us. For some these places need healing. For others the cross will bring direction or correction. For some it will be a revelation of mercy and for others a death.

1. Looking around, have you ever wondered if compromise is the only alternative for young people?

2. If you're a mother, how does this make you feel?

3. As a young woman how does this make you feel?

4. What about when it comes to your life?

5. Have you ever had other Christians tell you to calm down?

Without a doubt, compromise has become the standard in the majority of our culture. But it was never part of God's. He is ultimate in His stance.

Most of us might have a difficult time mixing the cross with our sexuality. The enemy has done an incredibly thorough job of separating God from the dynamic of love, intimacy, romance, and passion. It has only been of late that Christian voices everywhere are refuting this heinous fallacy.

Big Idea

The cross leaves no room for compromise.

6. Have you seen the war in the media and movies to separate God from the powerful area of sexuality?

7. When God is introduced in this realm, what does it look like?

8. Why do you think our culture tries so desperately to tie God to judgment and religion?

9. Did Jesus align Himself with the religious leaders of His time?

Why not?

My lover spoke and said to me, "Arise, my darling, my beautiful one, and come with me. See! The winter is past; the rains are over and gone." (Song 2:10–11)

10. How does this verse fly in the face of our culture's reasoning?

11. What does this verse speak to you?

12. Do you ever find yourself embarrassed by the dichotomy between the media's representation of Christianity and our reality of it?

"Whoever acknowledges me before men, I will also acknowledge him before my Father in heaven." (Matt. 10:32)

13. Have you ever been ashamed to admit you were a Christian?

14. Was it because you were ashamed of Christ or was it because you didn't want to be labeled as judgmental and hypocritical?

15. Did you compromise because you didn't want others to think you were uptight or out of step?

16. How did it make you feel the first time?

17. Did it get easier for you each time?

Regardless of your motivation . . . can you believe God is now offering you forgiveness and the power to stand strong where you once failed? If so, confess and receive it now.

HOLY MOMENT

Father,

Forgive and restore me now. Like Peter I have tried in my own strength and blown it. Wash me of guilt and fear. Forgive me for trying to walk in Your power without the cross. I choose now to embrace the power and forgiveness of the cross. I want it to be so much more than an object of jewelry in my life. Let it be emblazoned on my very being. So be it!

18. How is the cross vastly different from other religions or the law?

For he himself is our peace, who has made the two one and has destroyed the barrier, the dividing wall of hostility, by abolishing in his flesh the law with its commandments and regulations. His purpose was to create in himself one new man out of the two, thus making peace, and in this one body to reconcile both of them to God through the cross, by which he put to death their hostility. (Eph. 2:14–16)

19. Look at the preceding description of the work and power of the cross. What does it say the cross provided?

Other religions make you work to get the power, but the cross empowers. God knew we couldn't make it on our own. He answered with the life of His son. The cross provides peace, reconciliation, removal of barriers, abolished law, and His death made us one with God. What did the cross leave undone? Nothing.

20. The cross is so powerful . . . so why don't we speak of it more often?

We are to glory in the shame and foolishness of the cross. This symbol of death becomes our source of life. Too often we hear great preaching and teaching without a mention of the cross. But the first-century Christians understood it was the source of all life.

"You are the salt of the earth. But if the salt loses its saltiness, how can it be made salty again? It is no longer good for anything, except to be thrown out and trampled by men." (Matt. 5:13)

This is just one of five illustrations in the New Testament where Jesus talks about salt and saltiness. I have to admit I never really understood it until recently. I was at a conference and one of the speakers was exhorting us not to lose our saltiness by being negative. While she spoke I flashed back to chemistry class and saw the symbol for salt, NaCl+, I saw the vertical portion of the plus sign elongate until it was no longer an addition symbol but the sign of a cross. The Holy Spirit whispered, *Christians lose their saltiness when they preach a gospel or live a life void of the cross.* Without this positive ion the chemical compound commonly known as salt falls apart and in fact loses it saltiness.

Big Idea

The cross is the precursor to all true power.

Jesus set the example by choosing to endure the cross. We echo this whenever we say, "Not my will but Yours" (Luke 22:42). Embracing the cross is the precursor to all true power. It brings resurrection out of places of shame and death. How could we ever expect a resurrection when there has been no death?

> *Therefore, I urge you, brothers, in view of God's mercy, to offer your bodies as living sacrifices, holy and pleasing to God—this is your spiritual act of worship. (Rom. 12:1)*

21. What are the areas you have failed to present to the cross (the areas where you repeatedly fail, sexual or otherwise)?

22. Is thinking of sexuality as an offering to God difficult for you?

> *See that no one is sexually immoral, or is godless like Esau, who for a single meal sold his inheritance rights as the oldest son.*
> *Afterward, as you know, when he wanted to inherit this blessing, he was rejected. He could bring about no change of mind, though he sought the blessing with tears. (Heb. 12:16–17)*

Again, unrestrained appetites cause us to sell out or sell something precious as cheap. How often do we lose God's best because we wanted the immediate satisfaction?

23. Hebrews 12:16 ties sexual immorality to godlessness . . . why do you think this is so?

24. Do non-Christians find it confusing when Christians mess up sexually?

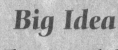

Christianity is a call to no longer live for temporal desires, but to live in the abundance of the Spirit. When Christians indulge in fleshly or worldly desires, it confuses everyone! This is especially disappointing when we know feasting the flesh ultimately yields no satisfaction. This is why we're admonished to live life in the Spirit, which is best described by the following verse.

Then he said to them all: "If anyone would come after me, he must deny himself and take up his cross daily and follow me." (Luke 9:23)

Lordship is not a one-time altar encounter, but a daily submission to His empowering truth. It is the exchange of one life for another.

25. If you have taken ownership or possession of something or someone, who makes the decisions? Since we were purchased, do we still have the right to make our own decisions?

26. How could you implement this truth into the dynamic of your daily life? (Give practical as well as spiritual examples.)

We err if we only emphasize the cross as a symbol of sacrifice—and miss its power. God wants those who have broken free from the rule of the flesh to discover freedom through the cross. It is where we leave the realm of "good" and truly become God's.

> *If we have been united with him like this in his death, we will certainly also be united with him in his resurrection. For we know that our old self was crucified with him so that the body of sin might be done away with, that we should no longer be slaves to sin—because anyone who has died has been freed from sin. Now if we died with Christ, we believe that we will also live with him. (Rom. 6:5–8, emphasis added)*

If we truly believe our life was hidden in Him, then His death freed us from the hold of sin and quickened us in Christ! Why emphasize death and neglect the life it offers us? This happens when we major on forgiveness and forget about the empowerment to walk free from sin (the go-and-sin-no-more dynamic).

Review Romans 6:11–14. In light of these verses, we could view grace as the condition of being dead to sin while alive in Him.

Big Idea

Obedience is our offering.

27. How does grace remove sin's mastery over our lives?

28. In light of this Scripture, what are we actually doing when we sin?

If we bring offerings to whatever we obey, it logically follows that what we obey has mastery over our life. The choice is ours: sin or righteousness.

The cross is about obedience, which is our daily offering.

29. In what areas do you need more power?

30. Do you spend more time asking for forgiveness or asking for the power not to blow it?

Remember the cross is a face-off. We need God's power, and I recommend various forms of fasting as a connection point for this.

Satan hates the cross. It mocks what he thought was victory. But he laughs when we try to live in our own strength and goodness. We are invited to drink living water; quench our thirst; dine; and then reside, remain, or abide in Him.

Big Idea

Without the cross we will try to live in the realm of "good"—and fail.

"I am the vine; you are the branches. If a man remains in me and I in him, he will bear much fruit; apart from me you can do nothing . . . As the Father has loved me, so have I loved you. Now remain in my love. If you obey my commands, you will remain in my love, just as I have obeyed my Father's commands and remain in his love." (John 15:5, 9–11)

This beautifully illustrates the relationship of Christ and His own; He is the Vine from which we draw life, nourishment and strength. He empowers us to bear fruit.

> *But the fruit of the Spirit is love, joy, peace, patience, kindness, goodness, faithfulness, gentleness and self-control. (Gal. 5:22–23)*

Big Idea

Communion invites us to be part of something bigger than us.

Communion represents the cross, for each time we partake we remember Christ's sacrifice.

31. Up until this point, what have your experiences with communion meant? (Be honest!)

In this chapter of *Kissed the Girls and Made Them Cry*, I shared how I'd taken communion without ever really connecting with its purpose. By offering His body and blood do you see how God wants to make this a point of connection for you?

32. How do we remain connected to the Vine?

33. According to Romans 12:1, we are urged to be pure in view of God's
_____, not_____. How is this Scripture
related to the act of communion?

34. How might communion have that kind
of powerful expression in your life?

Big Idea

*Obedience creates an
atmosphere for loving
communion.*

35. Is He merely one of many foods to dine on or is He our one and only source
of life?

36. God longs for those who want more than just to be _____ ;
    He desires those who want _____ .

37. What would that look like in your life, especially in the area of purity?

A HOLY MOMENT

Christ invites us to share "communion" with Him. He wants to lavish us with food that truly satisfies. Take a moment, pray, and ask God to show you what areas He wants to satisfy in your life. Would you be willing to take the time to allow the Holy Spirit to search your heart, and then take part in a personal time of communion of His body and blood?

Voice of a Daughter

Not only has He forgiven me my sin, but He's made me new! Completely new! He's poured grace and mercy on me, I'm just bathing in His loveliness! He's promised to make me strong, firm and steadfast. He going to make me all the things I need to be and all the things I've wanted to be for so long now.

–England

MAKE IT YOURS

Journal what He spoke in your communion time:

Song to Make It Real
From You

I will not make my boast
In the riches of gold
Or the wisdom and strength of my own
I will not place my trust
In the things of this life
For the One that I love is more

From You is everything
Through You I can live again
To You be the glory forevermore

In the cross I will boast
And my glory will be
In the One who left heaven for me
All my trust is secure
And my hope overflows
For the One that I love is more

From You
Through You
To You
Jesus

Glory, glory
All the glory
Glory to Your name

By Glenn Packiam, from the Desperation Band album *From the Rooftops*

© 2004 Vertical Worship Songs/ASCAP

Ten

BREAKING THE CURSE

Weighing Your Words

*R*ead chapter ten in *Kissed the Girls and Made Them Cry,* and view session four of "Purity's Power."

Voice of a Daughter

It is the first time I have felt clean, able to stand against the enemy without him having anything in me. That barrier is gone, thanks be to God!!! And I am free!!! Totally free! I'm not talking "abstinence." I'm talking freedom!!!

–U.S.A.

As we approach this chapter, it is important to establish the power of words. This is one way we're to walk like our heavenly Father. He is not only intentional with His words, but after their release He watches over His Word to perform it.

> *So is my word that goes out from my mouth: It will not return to me empty, but will accomplish what I desire and achieve the purpose for which I sent it. (Isa. 55:11)*

Words carry incredible power. They have the power to heal or wound, bless or curse, strengthen alliances or alienate friends. We've all experienced this on one level or another. I know I've been careless with words and brought wounding to others more often than I wished, and it's my earnest prayer to be more careful and deliberate in the purpose and intent of my words.

1. Why do you think God expects a return on His words?

2. Of course He knows the power in words. But how does God's Word return to Him?

I believe it returns when His children echo His Word and promises back to Him, thereby establishing them in their hearts. What could be accomplished if we passionately agreed with God's Word and set our hearts after His purpose? As humans our words are fallible, but not God's . . . they're infallible. We may or may not hit the mark, but He cannot miss. This is so certain we're told:

> *For no matter how many promises God has made, they are "Yes" in Christ. And so through him the "Amen" is spoken by us to the glory of God. (2 Cor. 1:20)*

3. What would happen if we actually believed our Father said "Yes" whenever it concerned His promises?

4. If you really believed your "Amen" or "So be it" actually brought glory to God, how would you approach the promises and warnings found in His Word?

I believe we'd actually recognize and realize a much more real and tangible level of the gravity, weight, or power found in the Word of God. Always keep in mind this fact: God is the Creator, and His words carry the power or seeds of creativity. They're released and reveal God. He said, "Let there be light!" and thus revealed a portion of Himself, because God is light. His Word is our connection to His will and His wondrous power in our lives.

This chapter will be woven in His will and Word. We will come in childlike faith and simply believe. As we release His Word, we in turn will be released.

Voice of a Daughter

This book has dramatically set me free from many lifelong bondages.

–U.S.A.

---

5. Think a moment: in which areas do you feel bound and in need of God's release?

6. Have you tried to release these areas only to have them come back around and entangle you again?

I have repeatedly referred to a present nightmare and God's greater dream. Now we're going to move away from the general and go more specific.

7. Have you ever suffered from a recurring nightmare?

8. If so, what were some of its elements? Explain.

Let's review the dynamics of blessings and curses in Chapter ten.

9. Read Deuteronomy 11:26–28 again. Under the Law, every blessing had a _____ attached to it if the command of the Lord was broken. So under the Law, your past mistakes and unlawful decisions would have brought a _____ on your life.
   But . . . Galatians 3:13–14 tells us that "_____ redeemed us from the _____ by becoming a curse for _____. He redeemed _____ in order that the _____ given to Abraham might come to the Gentiles (us) through _____.

10. Since Christ redeemed us from the curse, why do we still struggle against curses?

The answer is simple. Each and every promise is to be appropriated. Just as the children of Israel echoed "So be it," we appropriate the promises of God by faith.

Did Jesus die that none would perish? Yet daily thousands slip into eternity void of this salvation. Why?

It was never embraced in their lives. The Lordship and the "So be it" was never established.

The Christian life was never meant to be a casual accidental encounter, with a God who randomly drops things on us as He sees need or pleases. We are constantly invited to press in.

> *From the days of John the Baptist until now, the kingdom of heaven has been forcefully advancing, and forceful men lay hold of it. (Matt. 11:12)*

11. What does it mean to lay hold of something?

12. What are we being admonished to lay hold of?

This Scripture makes it evident serving God is not for the faint at heart. It must be advanced forcefully, and while it moves ahead we are to lay hold of it. We are to exercise the rights and dominion of children of the King while here on earth. We were never meant to cower before any foe of heaven. The very model of prayer is "Thy Kingdom come, thy will be done on earth as it is in heaven." There is to be a progressive restoration of all that was lost from the Fall, and we are to pursue this in the understanding that the heavens must retain our Lord Jesus until every enemy is made subservient to Him. This would mean we are to be active in rehearsing God's promise.

13. Looking at your family history, do you see any patterns of curses?

14. What are they?

It is quite possible these recurring tragedies or curses represent your version of the "dead men walking" slowly behind you. These may even appear as frightening images or voices from your past that show up uninvited in your dreams or thoughts.

> ### Voice of a Daughter
>
> *As I read and prayed the prayers, I got closer to an answer that I didn't even know I was looking for. Renouncing some soul ties I may have had and seeing the Lord longed to put to sleep what had been prematurely awakened started to set me free! It's different now. I don't even know how to explain it except the word "freedom."*
>
> –U.S.A.

15. Why is there no such thing as casual sex?

16. Define a soul tie.

17. Write down some examples of healthy soul ties.

18. Why is this knitting of souls in sexual encounters unhealthy outside of marriage?

You are ideally to be united with only one person sexually because it is reserved for the union of two who are one in the covenant of marriage. Intimacy must be exclusive for it to exist.

19. Without God's restoration, can two truly become one when they have already been sexually involved with others?

I believe they can *only* after repentance, healing, and restoration has taken place.

> *Marriage should be honored by all, and the marriage bed kept pure, for God will judge the adulterer and all the sexually immoral. (Heb. 13:4)*

To honor something is to add the weight of gravity to it. If something is not honored, it is esteemed lightly. Husbands can dishonor their wives just as wives can dishonor their husbands by not understanding this principle. This is one reason we find adultery rampant in our culture. Why would their sexual union be unique or intimate to them if they've already experienced sex with others?

It is the very reason people say, "Marriage is just a piece of paper." That is all it has become. Why would anyone think paper would add power? In a way they are right to think it does not! Honoring God's Word brings strength, covenant, and intimacy to marriage.

Think about this. If marriage means nothing, why are homosexuals fighting so hard to have theirs legitimized?

Paper will never make a heterosexual marriage legitimate; only God can make two one.

We honor our marriage before the wedding by remaining pure.

We honor our marriage after the wedding by never allowing others into it. Nor do we involve that which detracts from the beauty of sexual intimacy, such as pornography, masturbation, perversion, or impurity.

> ## Big Idea
> *Sex outside of marriage dishonors marriage, the individuals, and God, but sex in marriage honors God, the individuals, and marriage.*

Because I did not live these truths, I had to face off with many shadows. When I was married and should have been able to give myself freely, I found myself bound.

20. Have you wrestled with a lack of freedom because of images or guilt visits from your past?

21. If you were involved sexually before marriage . . . were these images an issue or did they spring up after you were married?

22. Read the bottom of page 116 and on to page 117 of *Kissed the Girls and Made Them Cry*. Do you want to be the beginning of a thousand generations who love God and keep His commandments? What curses would you like God to reverse in your family?

Even though there is always forgiveness, we often forget the dynamic of consequence.

23. Define the word *consequence*.

Choices we make are like seeds—some good, some bad. When we plant bad seeds, we can be forgiven, but this does not mean they will not grow and produce fruit in our lives. They will until they are confronted and uprooted. This is why it is so important to break soul ties and generational sins.

There is incredible hope and promise in the truth. We have Jesus as our example and the Holy Spirit as our guide. He is the One Job spoke of:

> *Even now my witness is in heaven; my advocate is on high. My intercessor is my friend as my eyes pour out tears to God; on behalf of a man he pleads with God as a man pleads for his friend.* (Job 16:19–21)

He is our Advocate, and even more, He is our Friend. He pleads on our behalf.

Now is your time to invite His presence and power to do this redemptive work in your life. Find a place where you can linger before Him undisturbed and lay hold of His covenant promises hidden in this simple prayer. You may want to incorporate worship music as you boldly come as His beloved before His throne. When you are ready, breathe this prayer.

In order to walk in purity, we must be whole, and only God by His Spirit can restore our broken places. Only He restores honor to our sexuality when there has been violation and dishonor. Only God can take the impure and defiled and make it holy and pure again. Only God can give us beauty for the ashes we bring Him.

We have a faithful and compassionate High Priest who knows us intimately. He is willing to pass His sword and cut away anything that holds you back from Him. He wants every unhealthy soul tie severed so only what is healthy will remain. He will send His Word to heal you and restore your soul.

Heavenly Father,

I come to You in the name of Jesus; I enter Your gates with thanksgiving and Your courts with a heart of praise. I'm overwhelmed by Your mercy and love for me, and I thank You in advance for the mighty work of redemption You will produce in my life.

Lord, God of heaven and earth, the great and awesome One, who keeps His covenant of love with those who love Him and obey His commands. Let Your ear now be attentive to the prayers of Your daughter. Let Your eyes watch over these words to perform them.

I confess my sins and the sins of my father's house; for every transgression known and unknown we've committed against You, forgive us. We've acted wickedly and been covered with shame because of our sins. But, You Lord are merciful and forgiving, even though we've rebelled against You and not obeyed the Lord our God or kept the laws given through His servants the prophets. We ask You to circumcise our hearts and roll away the sin, shame, and reproach of our sojourn in Egypt.

I confess and renounce my sin and the sins of my father's house for any and all involvement in the occult, witchcraft, or divination. (Pause here and remain sensitive to add anything the Holy Spirit might bring to your attention. Then specifically renounce these items or incidents before continuing. This may include, but is certainly is not limited to, astrology, séances, horror movies, games, books, etc.) *I renounce my involvement in it and break its curse off my life and off of every life that will pass through me. Bless my children as the generations stretch before You in love and obedience.*

I confess my sins and the sins of my father's house in the area of drug and alcohol abuse. Father, close now any door in the spirit this might have opened to sin, bondage, or oppression. I renounce my involvement (call the drugs by name if applicable) *and break the power of their curse off my life and off of every life that will pass through me. Bless my children as the generations stretch before You in love and obedience.*

Father, I confess and renounce my sin and the sins of my father's house for any and all involvement in sexual sin, impurity, perversion, adultery, homosexuality, and promiscuity. (Be sensitive here to specifically name the sins you are renouncing. Speak them out before Him without shame, for there is nothing hidden. He knows each of them and longs to remove their weight of guilt and shame from you. Then when you're ready proceed.)

Father, take the sword of Your Spirit and sever every ungodly sexual and emotional soul tie between me and . . . (Listen to the Holy Spirit and speak each name out as you hear it. It is quite possible you did not have intercourse with them but were sexually or emotionally entangled in a way reserved for your husband or Savior alone.)

After speaking each name, pray this:

Father, release Your angels to retrieve the fragments of my soul from these men (or women). Restore them to me by Your Spirit that I might be whole and holy again, set apart for Your pleasure.

I renounce my involvement in promiscuity or perversion and break the power of this curse off my life and off of every life that will pass through me. Barrenness is broken as You bless my children as the generations stretch before You in love and obedience.

(Place your hands on your eyes.)

Father, I renounce the hold of every perverted and promiscuous image. Forgive me for allowing vile and perverted images before me. I make a covenant according to Psalm 101:3 and I will guard the issues of my heart by way of the gateway of my eyes. I will not willingly allow any vile thing before my eyes. I renounce every unclean spirit and command it and its influence to go from my life.

Father, wash me in the cleansing blood of Jesus. For it alone has the power to cleanse and atone. I consecrate myself now as Your temple; by the power of Your Holy Spirit remove all defilement of my spirit, soul, and flesh from Your sanctuary. Fill me to overflowing with the indwelling of Your Holy Spirit. Open my eyes to see, my ears to hear, and my heart to receive all You have for me. I am completely Yours. Have Your way in my life. In the precious name of Jesus, amen.

Your name   Date

Feel free to remain silent and sensitive before Him a while. You may have experienced some coughing or a sensation of choking as you prayed and things were released and broken off your life. Do not let this frighten you, but allow it to serve as a confirmation of what God has accomplished. If none of this was experienced, do not trouble yourself about it either way.

(Ps.100:4; 2 Chron. 29:10–11; Neh. 1:5–7; Dan. 9:8–10; Josh. 5:9; Matt. 10:34; Heb. 4:12; 2 Chron. 29:5–6)

Note to Moms

I know you want a hope and a future for your daughter. I know you want her to inherit the promises and not your pain. Fast, and set a time apart to bring her before the Lord and break up the fallow ground through prayer so that even before she would go through this prayer process, her heart would be softened and ready.

HEALING IN HIS WINGS

Malachi chapter four tells us there is healing in His wings. Not only do I believe God wants to set you free . . . I believe He longs to heal you as well. As I wrote *Kissed the Girls and Made Them Cry*, the Holy Spirit posed this question: "What will you let Me do in your women's meetings?" I answered, "Lord, You can do whatever You want." He replied, "I want to heal My daughters. I want to cleanse not only the defilement of their spirits, I want to heal their diseases as well."

As far as God is concerned it does not have to be one or the other. It can be both. Nothing is too hard for Him and with Him the impossible becomes possible.

Drink in the following Psalm.

> *Praise the LORD, O my soul; all my inmost being, praise his holy name. Praise the LORD, O my soul, and forget not all his benefits who forgives all your sins and heals all your diseases, who redeems your life from the pit and crowns you with love and compassion, who satisfies your desires with good things so that your youth is renewed like the eagle's. (103:1–5, emphasis added)*

It admonishes us to "forget not" all His benefits. We are quick to major on and remember that He in fact forgives all our sins, but will we dare to believe He will heal all our diseases? Is a venereal disease exempt from the mercy of God? Is it perhaps a disease He refuses to heal because "we got what we deserved"? In light of this reasoning, do we in fact get what we deserve when we sin? No! We deserve judgment and receive mercy. I pray even now God will come and impart His healing power. It does not matter where you are . . . just as you embraced and received His forgiveness, even now embrace and receive His healing.

MY PRAYER FOR YOU

Heavenly Father,

I believe You long to heal not only the hearts but also the wombs of Your daughters. Come by Your love and might and take away our reproach and issues of blood. There was never one who came to You for healing that You did not touch. Even now touch Your daughters as they reach out. May Your virtue flow freely to cleanse and make them whole. To You alone be all the glory and praise.

YOUR RESPONSE

Heavenly Father,

I come to You in the name of Jesus, by the power of the Holy Spirit and say beyond a doubt I believe You have forgiven me of all—not just some—of my sins, and now, God, I choose not to forget the benefit of Your healing power as well. Come into my body, cleanse and heal my inmost being. Purge my body of any and all disease and wash me clean. I receive Your mercy and healing into my bloodstream and into every part of my innermost being and body.

Voice of a Daughter

I am 40, and had never felt pure in heart even though I was born-again at 26. I just couldn't shake my former lifestyle. As God revealed my impurities, I called them what they were, confessed what I'd done, repented each sin by name, and asked forgiveness. For the first time I felt soooo clean and with no shadow of shame!!! I am being restored to my former splendor!! I have all my pieces—nothing missing, nothing broken! Praise Jesus my Prince!!

—U.S.A.

Voice of a Son

I've just finished reading your book, and felt compelled to express my feelings of freedom and delight to finally see someone else with my values. I'm a 46-year-old male and was molested by my mother as a young child. Even though your intended audience was female, this book with its prayer passage and request for breaking the curses has begun to set me free!

–USA

Song to Make It Real

I Am Free!

Through You the blind will see
Through You the mute will sing
Through You the dead will rise
Through You all hearts will praise
Through You the darkness flees
Through You my heart screams I am free

I am free to run (echo)
I am free to dance (echo)
I am free to live for You (echo)
I am free (echo)

By Jon Egan, from the Desperation Band album *From the Rooftops*

© 2004 Vertical Worship Songs/ASCAP

MAKE IT YOURS

Journal your blessings and the curses you believe are broken:

_____

_____

_____

_____

_____

_____

_____

_____

_____

_____

_____

_____

_____

_____

_____

_____

_____

_____

_____

_____

_____

_____

_____

_____

_____

_____

_____

Eleven

CHOSEN BY A PASSIONATE, HOLY GOD

Escaping Faithless Love

*R*ead chapter eleven in *Kissed the Girls and Made Them Cry.*

Too often we are so excited about escaping judgment and bondage, we miss this deeper connection . . . it's about becoming "His."

> *"You yourselves have seen what I did to Egypt, and how I carried you on eagles' wings and brought you to myself."* (Ex. 19:4)

He rescues us for one purpose . . . to bring us to Himself.

Big Idea

God snatches us from faithless love to bring us to His everlasting arms.

1. How does this beautiful truth make you feel?

As already described, this verse is our rescue by Christ on the cross.

For he himself is our peace, who has made the two one and has destroyed the barrier, the dividing wall of hostility. (Eph. 2:14)

2. Have you ever been separated from, or at odds with, someone? There's a breach, and no matter how you try to make it better it only becomes worse? Cite the three things which need to happen for there to be restoration.

-

-

-

When these are confronted and restored, you can be with each other without being uncomfortable. You rejoice because you can be comfortable in each other's presence again!

If the joy of this dynamic exists in human restoration, how much more should there be cause to celebrate when the breach between the God of heaven and His daughters is repaired?

3. In light of this truth, what should be our response to salvation?

4. How does this fly in the face of what we most often think?

But just as he who called you is holy, so be holy in all you do; for it is written: "Be holy, because I am holy." (1 Peter 1:15–16)

To *be* something means it defines your very existence. We can *act* holy and not *be* holy; we can *look* holy and not *be* holy.

For he chose us in him before the creation of the world to be holy and blameless in his sight. (Eph.1:4 NIV)

5. Who does "in him" refer to?

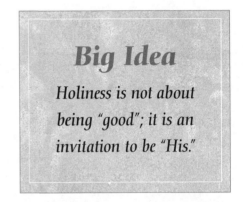

Big Idea

Holiness is not about being "good"; it is an invitation to be "His."

6.   Who does "in his sight" speak of?

Provision was made before mankind drew its first breath, for we inhabited His heart. If this is not intimacy, if this is not safety, what is? The dream was in place before the nightmare was foreshadowed. The enemy was confronted and defeated before the serpent even whispered in the Garden. God declared, "This daughter is mine . . . holy and blameless!"

7. Most of us understand the concept of *do*, because we are all so busy doing, but what does it mean to *be*?

But you are a chosen generation, a royal priesthood, a holy nation, a people belonging to God, that you may declare the praises of him who has called you out of darkness into his wonderful light. (1 Peter 2:9)

8. Examine this Scripture and break down the following terms and how we should relate to them.

- Chosen generation

- Royal priesthood

- Holy nation

- A people belonging to God

> **Big Idea**
>
> *Whether you realize it or not, you were never truly free.*

Holiness is about intimate relationship and covenant; we're no longer our own. You may initially recoil at the idea of someone laying claim to you. But let's look deeper by reviewing 1 Peter 2:10–11:

Once you were not a people, but now you are the people of God; once you had not received mercy, but now you have received mercy. Dear friends, I urge you, as aliens and strangers in the world, to abstain from sinful desires, which war against your soul.

Because of Adam's transgression, we were taken captive. If we spurn this sacrifice, we remain the dark prince's. You're free to choose who you belong to, but there is not a cosmic middle world.

Throughout the Scriptures, redemption is repeatedly compared to the union of a man and a woman.

Review the account of the Bridegroom and His bride found on pages 132–136 of *Kissed the Girls and Made Them Cry.*

9. We are His bride. How then should we respond to this great expense, commitment, and sacrifice?

10. How are you readying yourself?

I cannot emphasize enough the dynamic of worship as part of developing a lifestyle of readiness.

11. Did you know you were engaged?

The significance of the veiled bride echoes again the issue of separation from this world because of our covenant with the heavenly Prince.

12. How do you communicate who you belong to?

It is an awesome thing to be chosen by a Holy God who not only calls us to be more than we ever thought we could be, but loves us with more passion than we would ever believe we were worthy of!

13. Has the story of the bride and Bridegroom changed your perspective of the following Scripture?

> *In my Father's house are many rooms; if it were it not so, I would have told you. I am going there to prepare a place for you. And if I go and prepare a place for you, I will come back and take you to be with me that you also may be where I am. (John 14:2–3)*

14. List your insights here:

For some this means safety, or promise, but for most on one level or another it speaks of love. My dear friend Lisa always says, "Love prepares." There is something amazing in the fact the Prince of heaven even now prepares a place for you and me! He takes special time and care to design, decorate, and fill each room with just what you will need to feel loved. A place where you'll flourish!

This weekend I tackled a portion of my sons' room. They'd worked hard to clean and organize it, and with this accomplished there was opportunity to surround them with something more. We rearranged the furniture and added a cozy chair in a sunny corner. Why? I wanted their room to say "I love you!" every day!

*Husbands, love your wives, just as Christ loved the church and gave himself up for her . . .
"For this reason a man will leave his father and mother and be united to his wife, and the two
will become one flesh." . . . This is a profound mystery—but I am talking about Christ and the
church. (Eph. 5:25, 31–32)*

15. In light of this Scripture, how important is it the husband loves his wife first
    and foremost?

If God chose marriage as the earthly example
of Christ's relationship with the church, He
never meant it to be a place of abuse or pain.
God never set women up to be abandoned, neglected, or abused. He loves them.

16. Do you see why two men or two
    women can never really truly be
    married, no matter what earthly courts
    may say?

> **Big Idea**
>
> *Never forget, truth
> overrides man's law,
> just as intimacy
> displaces rules.*

HOLY MOMENT

*Heavenly Father,
I don't want the promises without first knowing the You, my Promiser. You are
more than enough for me. Veil me in the Spirit so I am Yours. I leave behind the
realm of good and step into the intimacy of being God's.*

Song to Make It Real
Treasure

Your breath is like rain
Your Word it sustains me
I've come to this place
With intentions of finding You

Your truth is a lamp
Your wisdom my light
I'm seeking Your face
With intentions of finding You

I would run for a thousand years
If I knew every step would be getting me closer
I'd swim to the ocean floor
For my Lord is the treasure
My Lord is the treasure

Holy holy
Holy is the Lord

Holy my God is holy
Holy is the Lord

All the angels sing
Holy Jesus is holy
Holy is the Lord

My Lord is the treasure
My Lord is the treasure
My Lord is the treasure
My Lord is the treasure

By Jared Anderson, from the Desperation Band album *From the Rooftops*

© 2004 Vertical Worship Songs/ASCAP

Voice of a Daughter

It has changed a lot of my preconceived ideas on marriage. It has softened my heart like never before, and has brought me to a new and unique level with Jesus. Since reading the book I don't mind it when guys open doors for me. I won't be afraid to submit to my future husband. I have a greater respect for marriage. Mind-sets of the world have been blown completely away.

–U.S.A.

MAKE IT YOURS

Journal your longing to be swept away into His presence.

_____
_____
_____
_____
_____
_____
_____
_____
_____
_____
_____
_____
_____
_____
_____
_____
_____

Twelve

THE POWER OF PURITY

Leaving the Realm of Excuses

*R*ead chapter twelve in *Kissed the Girls and Made Them Cry.*

Daughters, don't let anyone look down on you because you're young, but set an example for believers male and female, young and old, in speech, in life, in love, in faith, and in purity (1 Tim. 4:12, author paraphrase).

1. Why does this admonition seem contradictory?

2. Are we empowering the youth to walk in this?

3. What empowers us?

Voice of a Daughter

I heard your "Purity's Power" CDs one night with my cousin. We stayed up until 4:30 A.M.! They're truly wonderful!! My walk with God deepened and I was challenged in so many ways! Thank you so much!!!

—U.S.A.

---

4. What do you hear in her comments?

I hear excitement, and hope. You can almost hear her say, "Thanks for believing I could make it!" Women young and old are willing to raise the bar when it comes to purity. We need to give them some inspiration! They don't want a list of rules—they want the hope of beauty!

Big Idea

Truth sets us free, grace empowers, but excuses and fear rob us.

Voice of a Daughter

I read the book and was so encouraged! I was able to stop bad sins in my life before they got a serious hold over me. I was challenged and grew so much deeper in God as a result!! Thank you for being open, loving and caring about us!!

—U.S.A.

We should never be afraid to boldly declare transforming truths. Why remain silent when every other voice screams its perversion?

5. Explain the difference between holiness and purity?*

Big Idea

The truth confronts lies, stopping them before they get out of hand and produce fruit.

"You have loved righteousness and hated wickedness; therefore God, your God, has set you above your companions by anointing you with the oil of joy." (Heb. 1:9)

6. How does this Scripture link our reactions to righteousness and wickedness and their effect on our anointing and joy?

7. How are we to respond to those involved in wickedness?

Jesus did not hate sinners. This Scripture represents what should be our aversion to our own lack of righteousness or wickedness. Whether this is in word, deed, motive, or the off-color jokes we laugh at, God is asking us to let holiness develop purity and discern wickedness. He invites us to confront both the secret and public ones in order to be examples of godliness. I've been grieved as I felt the weight of compromise I've encouraged in others. (If you haven't experienced this, great . . . it's not a fun feeling!)

There is incredible promise in this . . . God is looking for those He can anoint with His Spirit and joy! It is those who choose to call Him their portion and reward. David pleased God because he set his heart on pursuing God and His desires.

> ## Big Idea
>
> *How we relate to God is more important than anything we imagine we do for Him! He wants to be our intimate and ultimate pursuit.*

"Here is my servant whom I have chosen, the one I love, in whom I delight." (Matt. 12:18)

The Spirit of the LORD will rest on him—the Spirit of wisdom and of understanding, the Spirit of counsel and of power, the Spirit of knowledge and of the fear of the LORD—and he will delight in the fear of the LORD. (Isa. 11:2–3)

Note to Moms

Ask questions. Don't be afraid to debrief your daughter as you face situations in and out of the home. We are all bombarded by a nonstop onslaught of perversion, promiscuity, and an all-out attack on our true value as women. Don't hesitate to ask how this makes her feel.

8. In your own words, what does it mean to delight in the fear of the Lord?

According to Scripture, *the fear of the Lord* is to love what God loves and hate what He hates. It is to honor Him in all we do . . . to tremble at the beauty of His Word and call it our delight.

Big Idea

We delight in God . . .
God delights in us!

9. Why are we only to examine ourselves and not others?

10. How do we examine ourselves?

11. When we invite the Holy Spirit to weigh our actions and motives, what instrument does He use in this process?

For the word of God is living and active. Sharper than any double-edged sword, it penetrates even to dividing soul and spirit, joints and marrow; it judges the thoughts and attitudes of the heart. Nothing in all creation is hidden from God's sight. Everything is uncovered and laid bare before the eyes of him to whom we must give account. (Heb. 4:12–13)

12. Is surgery ideally performed in dim or bright light?

> ## Big Idea
>
> *God's sword is forged of living, penetrating light. It has the power to divide what we cannot.*

13. Are surgical scalpels dull or sharp?

Never fear the brightness of truth or the dual-edged sword. Both are precisely forged for accuracy and speed. They will quickly have their way if we yield and do not struggle under their penetration.

14. Can you embrace and believe the power of this truth?

HOLY MOMENT

Invite the Word now to watch over you and dance in your heart. Ask the Holy Spirit to open your ears so you can hear it speak in the night watches.

15. Have there been times when the Word spoke to you and you did not know?

16. Write the Scriptures, songs, or words breathed into you as you open up to this:

There's a death threat on truth. Our culture has twisted and distorted God's wisdom and replaced it with its own set of standards, but it is foolish nonsense that changes each decade. In contrast, God's Word endures forever.

> For, "All men are like grass, and all their glory is like the flowers of the field; the grass withers and the flowers fall, but the word of the Lord stands forever." (1 Peter 1:24–25)

17. What does this Scripture liken us to?

> ## Voice of a Daughter
>
> *I'm 19 years old this year and I just wanted to say Lisa's book transformed my life! A friend gave it to me recently while I was experiencing a dry spell in my spiritual life. It showed me the power of purity, and Jesus broke the yoke of impurity in my life. I no longer find myself struggling with unclean thoughts.*
>
> *—Singapore*

18. Ultimately what will happen to our "fifteen minutes of fame"?

19. What standard will we answer to?

20. Does God take into account our cultural influences?

> ## Big Idea
>
> *The Word is alive and active. It longs to dance in your heart and whisper to you in the night watches.*

Often when lies are prevalent, purity seems impossible or unrealistic . . . it's not. It's a lie to believe He's incapable when He promised to keep us from falling and present us blameless.

In truth this is the way it should be:

> *But among you there must not be even a hint of sexual immorality, or of any kind of impurity, or of greed, because these are improper for God's holy people.* (Eph. 5:3, emphasis added)

21. How does this compare with the reality of today?

22. Examining yourself by the light of this Word . . . are there areas where you're hinting?

23. Why?

24. What happens when we hint?

As God's we should honor Him in all we say and do. We're more than forgiven—we're His. We are light where we were once darkness. Let's review this Scripture in Ephesians:

> *Nor should there be obscenity, foolish talk or coarse joking, which are out of place, but rather thanksgiving. (5:4)*

25. Too often we fail to realize the meaning of these words. Define the following:

    Obscenity:

    Foolish talk:

    Coarse joking:

26. How common are these?

Paul continues:

> *For of this you can be sure: No immoral, impure or greedy person—such a man is an idolater—has any inheritance in the kingdom of Christ and of God. Let no one deceive you with empty words, for because of such things God's wrath comes on those who are disobedient. Therefore do not be partners with them. (Eph. 5:5–7)*

In case we didn't get it, Paul is giving context to this warning. The immoral, impure, or greedy are idolaters without an inheritance in the kingdom of Christ or of God.

27. What do you think Paul meant by "let no one deceive you with empty words"?

28. What are empty words?

29. Give an example of some.

These words have no real power to effect change, but they do have the power to deceive you into complacency.

Don't you know that friendship with the world is hatred toward God? (James 4:4)

30. How do you feel about this Scripture?

Big Idea

Truth inspires us to rise to God's perspective and way.

31. Is this how Jesus positioned Himself?

The world has a voice and fellowship; we're not to fit in but to be transformed by the renewing of our minds. This present age invites us to believe whatever we like as long as we'll blend in and enjoy the world.

Voice of a Daughter

There is no point in covering over the real issues, my generation have been out there, done it all and needs honesty and straight talk to get things dealt with. If no one ever talks about what has really happened and how to get set free then how are we meant to know anything is wrong and how these undealt areas may be affecting our relationship with Jesus and others?

–New Zealand

---

32. Where does sin begin, according to James 1:14–15?

Having lost all sensitivity, they have given themselves over to sensuality so as to indulge in every kind of impurity, with a continual lust for more. (Eph. 4:19)

The term, *given themselves over,* describes a surrender or yielding of the will to the demands or wishes of another.

33. Have there been places where you've yielded your position of purity only to find your adversary more powerful in the next encounter?

Yielding to sexual sin is like throwing another log on the fire. Lust's flames threaten to rage out of control! As our senses dull, we lose our sensitivity to the Spirit and become driven by the sensory realm. Each act of indulgence reinforces lust and strengthens its stronghold or fortress of habits.

Voice of a Daughter

Masturbation became a way of life, and the more I did it the more I was driven, even turning to pornography to feed my need.

–Canada

I do not believe masturbation fosters purity, and it works against our ultimate desire to walk pure before a holy God. It attempts to meet valid human needs in an invalid way and can lead us down a path of selfishness and lust. I am not saying it is sin, but it is a shadow. It is not for children of the light to walk in shadows. Most sex addicts or couples wrestling with dysfunction have lust, selfishness, or masturbation as core issues, even after marriage.

The need is valid, but the way they choose to meet it is counterproductive to purity and intimacy.

True intimacy must be reciprocal rather than self-focused.

34. How does masturbation work against intimacy?

35. How does pornography work against intimacy?

36. Are homosexual interactions an example of intimacy?

The body is not meant for sexual immorality, but for the Lord, and the Lord for the body. By his power God raised the Lord from the dead, and he will raise us also. (1 Cor. 6:13–14)

Christ's resurrection from the dead released us from the power of sexual sin.

Put to death, therefore, whatever belongs to your earthly nature: sexual immorality, impurity,lust, evil desires and greed, which is idolatry. Because of these, the wrath of God is coming. (Col. 3:5–6)

Each of you should learn to control his own body in a way that is holy and honorable. (1 Thess. 4:4)

37. Does this Scripture apply only to the single?

38. If you are married, how could this be incorporated into your marriage?

39. In light of this, how then should we live?

Marriage should be honored by all, and the marriage bed kept pure, for God will judge the adulterer and all the sexually immoral. (Heb. 13:4)

40. If you are married, what does this Scripture speak to you?

Big Idea

The cross is a place of mercy, death, and power, not indulgence.

41. What are unnatural desires and indecent acts usually the result of?

42. Why is pornography a violation of purity?

43. What Scripture admonishes us to put pornography away from us?

44. How does pornography affect a marriage?

> # Big Idea
> *Purity of thought produces purity of action, appearance, and conversation.*

45. How does it affect men's perception of women?

46. How does it affect women's perception of themselves?

We'll falter if we haven't inwardly won the war. Sin begins in thought and is spurred by desire. The mind is where we win or lose the battle.

HOLY MOMENT

Father,
I wrestle not with flesh and blood. Make me strong in the power of Your might. To do this I want Your truth in every area of my life.

Song to Make It Real

Willingly

Like the dew comes to the morning
We will come to You
Captivate us with Your beauty
'Til all we want is You
This is what we're living for
This is our reward
To see the nations worship You
We will give our all

We say yes Lord
We say yes Lord
We say yes Lord
We willingly come

From every tribe they come to You
And gather round Your throne
This is the great multitude
The ones You made Your own
This is what we're living for
This is Your reward
To see the nations worship You
We will give our all

I wanna go where You're going Jesus
I wanna say what You're saying Lord
I wanna do what You're doing Jesus
I am Yours

By Glenn Packiam, from the Desperation Band album *From the Rooftops*

© 2004 Vertical Worship Songs/ASCAP

Voice of a Daughter

This country has gone so far on this issue that it is now commonplace to see all sorts of things on TV, the Internet, and magazines that should absolutely not be there. I personally would like to thank you on behalf of people in this generation for bringing new light to this subject.

–U.S.A.

MAKE IT YOURS

Journal any questions you need the Holy Spirit to answer for you.

_____

_____

_____

_____

_____

_____

_____

_____

_____

_____

_____

_____

_____

_____

_____

_____

_____

_____

_____

_____

_____

_____

Thirteen

DRESSED TO KILL

Dressing Your Part

*R*ead chapter thirteen in *Kissed the Girls and Made Them Cry,* and view session two of *Purity's Power.*

Voice of a Daughter

We watched the video "Packaging Is Power" last week and it caused a lot to be brought to the surface, mainly heart motives and old behaviour patterns and mindsets. We had a great discussion about why we wear what we do, how to maintain individuality and our God-given personality whilst being modest and bringing God glory. When I first got saved I dressed for men and to make women jealous, so I had issues.

—New Zealand

I love the honesty here. How many of us dress for men and to intimidate women? How many of us dress for women and to intimidate men? These are questions only we can answer.

> *Dress the part . . . unless you don't want it.*
>
> —Kenneth Cole

An inspired sister sent this quote and I put it up in my office. It got me thinking. It's an awesome representation of what we are talking about . . . what exactly is the part we're dressing for?

Big question: Have we given our young girls images of females clothed in purity, beauty, and dignity? Do we older women have any?

I am not even sure we'd know what it looked like. Look at the images women young and old have to choose from. To gain perspective, let's consider the world's a stage . . . what's our role?

I know there are many boxes and categories the world tries to cram us in, but what part do you want to play? This dynamic does not go away with age. It is something we should revisit as the seasons of our life shift one into another. Think of it, God chose you before the beginning of time for a purpose, a plan, a role.

> *All the days ordained for me were written in your book before one of them came to be.*
> (Ps. 139:16)

God has woven you into His beautiful story. This makes it so much more than a modesty issue . . . it becomes a matter of purpose and intent. Pause a moment and think about this.

1. If you could live your dream role and restructure your image and presentation by means of your own supernatural extreme makeover . . . what would you inspire?

2. What story would you want to tell?

3. Describe how you would choose to be if you could rewind your current image. How would people describe you?

She's strong!

She's beautiful.

She's feminine.

She's fun.

She's elegant.

How about this one . . . she's free!

Never let anyone tell you Christian women should be anything less than a shining representation of the above. Think of the opposite of these: weak, ugly, masculine, boring, cheap, and bound. Yuck! Not how any of us want to be described.

4. But be honest . . . how does the world describe Christian women?

5. Why do you think this is?

We have the power to change this. Are you willing to play your part? Actors spend a lot of time studying their characters so they are believable in their roles. Let's look at the godly examples we have to gain insight. Review Genesis 12:11, 14; 24:16; 26:7; and 29:17.

6. What did the world say about the godly daughters of promise in the days of Abraham?

7. What are your thoughts on this?

8. In the eyes of these ancients there was a link between godliness and beauty. Why is it so different now?

In those ancient days, women made and designed their own clothing. Their garments expressed their individuality rather than designer preferences. Garments were intimately linked to the wearer—perhaps your mother or grandmother made it for you or with you. They would have been appalled at the concept of wearing strangers' names on their personal clothing. Things have changed, but just because most of us don't make our own clothing, it doesn't mean we have to lose our individuality. As I travel I am challenging women worldwide to enter the fashion industry and reclaim this realm of beauty.

Be realistically inspired and begin to collect pictures for your collage at the end of this chapter. I want a dream you can capture. (If you're forty don't frustrate yourself with images of girls barely fifteen wearing outfits only they can wear.) Gather lots of images ranging from clothing, boots, shoes, purses, scarves, jewelry, friends, mothers embracing children, and grandmothers smiling at their legacy.

EXTREME WARDROBE MAKEOVER

This is meant to be constructive and fun. Enlist a friend who is willing to confront these issues with you. After you've each clearly outlined and described how you want to represent yourself, spend time in each other's closet. Tell her which of her outfits are your favorites and why. What colors make her radiant?

Then bravely attack the rest. If she has something that is just not her . . . tell her so. What does she wear that is working against her, and what is working for her? Go through her closet item by item. (I find it easiest to pull it all out first so you can see what you are dealing with.) You'll each find a number of items you no longer wear that can be given away to others in need.

Then it's time for your closet.

As you purge, ask questions of each other.:

Does this communicate who I am accurately?

When was the last time you wore this?

Why have you kept it?

Everyone needs a sweat suit, but if they're your whole wardrobe there's an issue. (Believe me I drive kids to school in them.)

If you need help, there are a number of great books on decluttering your closet, but just do it! It may take two days but you will feel freer when it is done.

Voice of a Daughter

There were times I really felt like a nonperson while I was in this transition. I suddenly felt like a boring, Christian, sack cloth wearing nonperson—UNTIL He changed my heart and showed me some things and gave me a totally new and wonderful and unique style which I really like and it's the real me. I love being feminine now, without being "fruffy"—that was a new American word for us down under.

–Down Under

9. We are communicating, whether or not words are spoken. What three forms of communications were listed in Chapter 13?

   •

   •

   •

"Man looks at the outward appearance, but the LORD looks at the heart."
(1 Sam. 16:7)

10. Is God saying this is wrong?

11. How could initial, visual responses protect us?

> # Big Idea
>
> *There is no getting around it . . . people are influenced by what they see more than by what they hear.*

This is even truer for men than women because they are very sight oriented.

12. In light of this . . . what are we communicating to the men?

13. What kind of responses are we encouraging?

14. Women have incredible power to influence . . . are we using this wisely?

15. Are we inspiring men or conspiring with their flesh?

16. Are we empowering them to be more? Or reducing them to their base level?

17. How do mixed messages confuse and frustrate everyone?

18. Have you ever misrepresented your intent by word or action and had a really hard time recovering your position of original intent?

I know I have then wondered how I could be more careful and effective next time. As women of passion, purity, and power it will always be easier to position ourselves correctly rather than recover lost ground.

How you present yourself communicates an immediate message and often an implication.

19. What is the initial impression you wish to communicate?

20. How are you affecting other women with your clothing?

21. Are you encouraging males in godly thought patterns or desires?

22. Are you encouraging other women in godly thought patterns, or are you threatening or intimidating them? Exercise for the brave . . . ask a friend what she feels you are saying.

Voice of a Daughter

I have never looked better and I give God the glory, because I am now clothed with strength and honour, I am clothed with Him and the anointing is better any day than anything the world can come up with. All the hardness is gone, sin really contorts people and changes them physically, but allowing Jesus to get involved in your wardrobe and overall appearance, while He's doing the work on the inside is the best makeover possible.

–New Zealand

Modesty is also about not *bragging* or *showing off* as well as having the right amount of coverage for the setting and relationship you're in.

23. Do people see you, or only what you are wearing?

Big Idea

As children of God, everything is ultimately about honoring our Father.

24. What are the things you would only want to reveal to your husband who you know loves you and will never leave?

It is good and godly to be intimate with your husband, but this is a very different level of intimacy than what you have with a boyfriend . . . no matter how much you love him.

We can be fashionable and attractive without being fashioned into a worldly image.

25. Why is it easier to deal in extremes (dress codes) or lists of rules?

> **Big Idea**
> *Intimacy levels should never exceed our trust level.*

26. How might your manner of dress betray what you trust in?

27. Do you recognize groups segregated by dress style or even brands?

> **Big Idea**
> *Naked is not necessarily intimate; sometimes it's just naked.*

28. List a few groups and describe how they present themselves:

29. Does dress and appearance accurately locate you?

You must know this about God . . . He loves diversity! Just look at creation. Christian women should not look like clones . . . we should be as diverse as the bounty of our Creator.

We have managed to become bored with breasts. We've seen them everywhere and from every angle, and now they're boring. What's a culture to do? Let's inflate them! Let's make them so big and high they no longer bore us! Let's totally forget their original intent and go for the outrageous! Where will all this end?

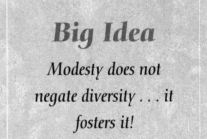

Big Idea

Modesty does not negate diversity . . . it fosters it!

30. Talk to someone a generation older than you, and ask them how they look at all this. Record their response:

31. Do you know someone who has her own style?

Young:

Middle-aged:

Senior:

32. How does this make you feel about her?

33. What is unique about you or your style?

34. What does it tell others about you?

We should use this power to our advantage and communicate our intentions effectively. We don't want to send mixed messages and in the end sabotage what we really wanted to say.

Too often women confuse being conquered with power. It's not like lust-filled men are asking us to share their lives.

The real issue here is not sexual. It is ultimately a question of honor.

> **Big Idea**
>
> *We're mistaken when we equate our ability to inspire lust with personal empowerment.*

35. What is the deeper struggle represented here?

36. How far are we from presenting an image of widespread whoredom?

> **Big Idea**
>
> *The very image of "woman" is under attack.*

37. Describe the media-propagated image that wars against women:

38. What has been the by-product of this? (anorexia, bulimia, suicide, etc.)

> **Big Idea**
>
> *Blatant, aggressive, in-your-face seduction threatens males. They sense a challenge, and testosterone levels rise to meet it.*

39. What inheritance and reality are we leaving our daughters?

40. Do you agree the way we attract a guy is the way he'll expect to be maintained?

41. How might the choice to wear something suggestive betray what you really think of yourself?

42. Our culture promises women more power as they reveal more. Do you believe this? Why or why not?

Voice of a Daughter

I am now dressing as God's daughter would dress and acting as such. I'm gaining wisdom and strength each and every day.

–U.S.A.

43. I have heard a lot of young women say, "It is my choice to dress however I want. If guys struggle with it, that's their issue, not mine!" According to God's Word, are we free to embrace this type of reasoning? If not, why?

HOLY MOMENT

Do you find it easy to honor God except when it comes to dress? Why do you think that is? Take some time to honestly reflect on this. Ask God for the desire to honor Him in everything.

Voice of a Daughter

Talk about getting right to it—motives mean so much, and I know every day I have to check my own heart to make sure I am dressed a certain way that will bring Jesus glory rather than seeking my own. Then there is the balance of still wanting to look nice and feel good about yourself but not look like a granny with no individuality . . . thank goodness for the Holy Spirit who helps in all of these things.

—New Zealand

Collage

Make a collage of clothes and images that express who you are and what you want to communicate. After all, you are in command of the wardrobe for your role.

Song to Make It Real
For Your Name

Jesus Your name is far above all others
Jesus Your name be praised
No other name is worthy of all honor
Jesus Your name be praised

For Your name for Your glory
For the Lamb who once was slain
For the joy that's set before me
I will give my life away

For Your name
Kingdoms will fall and all will fade away
Jesus Your name is great
We become small so all the earth will see You
Jesus Your name is great

For the glory of Your name
I will give my life away
For the glory of Your name
I will give my life away

I will give my life away
I will give my life away
I will give my life away
I will give my life away
For Your name

By Glenn Packiam, from the Desperation Band album, *From the Rooftops*

© 2004 Vertical Worship Songs/ASCAP

fourteen

LIVING FREE FROM REGRET

Rebuilding the Broken Places

*R*ead chapter fourteen in *Kissed the Girls and Made Them Cry*.

Voice of a Daughter

I was in a relationship that took me to places I didn't want to go. Deception slowly seeped into my life and stole everything . . . my virginity, my dignity, and my innocence were ripped from my hands. A life that once overflowed with joy and was clothed with beauty was stripped bare and laid vulnerable, all devoured in the name of pleasure. I feared my body, spirit, and soul would never again experience the favor of God.

As I sat among the ruins of my life, I cried out, my heart full of grief and repentance. God reached out to me, but fear and shame would not allow me to receive His love. Then the voice of my Father whispered, "If you don't see yourself as forgiven, then why did I send my Son to die for you?" At that moment hope was breathed into my parched spirit. He was with me. He saw where I'd been and where I was now and in His presence, He rebuilt the ruins of my life into something beautiful.

–U.S.A.

As I read these words my heart is stirred by God's goodness, and I am reminded of His overwhelming love and forgiveness. He only asks that we turn to Him giving our whole hearts. As you know, I am well acquainted with both ruin and restoration. I long for others to learn from my pain and be healed or kept from their own.

1. How do we live free from regret?

To live free from regret you have to choose to live life on purpose. This means having an eye toward the future. To do this you must have a destination in mind.

By definition, regret carries guilt, remorse, and shame. It is an emotion with incredible capacity for repetitive and untold pain. It shrouds us with discouragement in an attempt to sink our souls into despair and hopelessness. You hear it often in phrases preceded by, "If only . . ."

2. We all have experienced "If only" sometime in our life. Why less apparent in childhood?

3. What is the correlation between regret and immediate consequences?

4. How does discipline purge us of guilt?

When my children were little, I overheard them talking to each other, "You better just tell her the truth, because Mom will find out one way or another." As children our consciences are tender toward our parents. We don't want to do anything to displease them, but somewhere along the way this childlike desire to please our Father can be lost.

He wants to give each of us the gift of repentance to replace our regret and shame and exchange the "fear of Mom or Dad" with the "fear of the Lord."

> *In mercy and truth atonement is provided for iniquity;*
> *And by the fear of the LORD one departs from evil.* (Prov. 16:6 NKJV)

HOLY MOMENT

Ask the Father in Jesus' name to impart by His Holy Spirit the revelation of the fear of the Lord. Pray it now.

Father, I thank you for Your mercy and faithfulness for my past. Impart to me now the revelation of the fear of the Lord. Let it swallow up the fear of judgment in my life, and draw me into Your holiness and presence. Amen.

Far too often regret goes deeper and lives longer than mere cause and effect. It continues to echo in our lives until it is finally addressed head-on.

5. Without the fear of the Lord, what do we become skilled in during our youth?*

> ## Big Idea
> *Mercy and truth cover our past, while the fear of the Lord guards our future.*

6. How does our response to choices change as we progress from childhood to youth?*

7. How does this change again as we mature from youth to adulthood?*

8. Why is this?

9. What heart condition fosters this?

If we are immersed in the Word of God it becomes our light that exposes darkness that would otherwise go undetected.

Think of something you recently did that you now regret. (It does not have to be sexual.)

10. Was there a consequence, or did the Holy Spirit convict you of your actions?

11. What was your response?

My son, do not despise the LORD*'s discipline and do not resent his rebuke, because the* LORD *disciplines those he loves, as a father the son he delights in. (Prov. 3:11–12)*

God's rebuke is good and not a sign of rejection, or even police action, but of His love. Our response to it reflects the hardness or tenderness of our heart.

Regret is also capable of following quickly. Something said or done yesterday in secret suddenly appears unexpected and uninvited today. Thoughtless words, careless deeds, and passing comments are always weighed heavier when repeated. They are often distorted as they gain weight with each repetition. In the light of today, our words or actions sound harsher or look glaringly different than they did in yesterday's soft focus and intentions. We find ourselves wanting to defend them, but somehow now they seem indefensible. "I didn't mean it that way. You don't understand. It was different then."

> # Big Idea
>
> *Regret will always be our portion when we live for the moment without weighing our words or deeds before giving them life.*

I experienced regret because I did not really believe the things I share with you. I thought I could outsmart it and never pay the piper. I mistakenly thought carefully cloaked deeds would never have any lingering effect.

Voice of a Mother

I have a 13-year-old daughter for whom I want the very best, but do not have the past example to show her. Your book empowered me to educate my daughter the way I was not. I have always known that rules have always been something youth like to test, so the truths and "relationship" examples in your book appear to be better methods of instilling a true value-system that she can embrace for herself.

–U.S.A.

Voice of a Mother

I picked up Kissed the Girls and Made Them Cry *so I could use it with my teenage daughter, but the Lord used it to heal so much in me first! I fasted and prayed through the book and was healed of so much guilt. Now, I'm ready to use it with my teenager. Thank you.*

–U.S.A.

As daughters who have become mothers, grandmothers, aunts, or loving big sisters and friends, we have an opportunity to pass on a legacy of learning and power rather than foolishness and victimization.

This means we should confess the sins of our past in this present so others may hear and learn.

This is an invitation for those who've known regret to shine light on their once-dark paths so others will not walk there. We are to warn others who now consider the path of promiscuity, "*Steer clear! The price is too high, and the interest compounds with time.*"

This can serve as reinforcement for you who've chosen to walk wisely. You may not have ever experienced sexual regret, but more than likely you've experienced its sting in another area. You have chosen well, and may the tears on these pages water the seeds of godliness you've sown.

I have lived long enough to find this true. It is backed by the following Scriptures:

> *For there is nothing hidden that will not be disclosed, and nothing concealed that will not be known or brought out into the open.* (Luke 8:17)

Big Idea

Each generation has the opportunity and mandate to redeem its mistakes by speaking truth and warning to the next.

But all things that are exposed are made manifest by the light, for whatever makes manifest is light . . . See then that you walk circumspectly, not as fools but as wise. (Eph. 5:13, 15 NKJV)

12. What is the resounding lesson in each of these verses?

> **Big Idea**
>
> *Only the truth empowers the next generation to walk in more . . . not the details, just the truth!*

Let's define what it means to live circumspectly. It is living with the constant realization our whole life is connected. The time will come when events from our past catch up to us in our future.

13. Describe an opportunity you or a friend had to live circumspectly and didn't, and the consequences that followed:

> **Big Idea**
>
> *There is ultimately really no such thing as a secret.*

14. Describe an opportunity or an event where you chose to be "circumspect" in your approach and how a crisis was averted.

15. Which event left you feeling empowered?

16. I am afraid most of us (especially if we're young) really don't believe our choices or secrets follow us. Why do you think this is so?

There were times when consequences and regret seemed delayed or even denied their right in my life. It was then that I labored under the false idea I'd somehow tricked God and would not reap what I had in fact sown . . . I was of course painfully wrong.

Do not be deceived: God cannot be mocked.
A man reaps what he sows. (Gal. 6:7)

Big Idea

Everything comes full circle.

Never once in my wild phase did I imagine the pain I'd experience some twenty years later when my two oldest sons asked, "Mom, you were a virgin when you married Dad . . . right?"

It was a life-defining moment for me. Their sweet voices did not accuse. They were attempting to affirm my virtue. In collegiate moments of passion I never even dreamed such questions existed. I made the decision, if there was no such thing as a secret, I wanted to be the one who told mine!

Too often we only look at the inviting portions of things, the way it looks, the way it feels, and the pleasure and happiness we deserve now! Only later when we check our backside we experience embarrassment.

Note to Moms

Anything less than honest answers will undermine the power of our children to walk in purity. You are released from giving details, for it is possible to tell truth without full disclosure.

Voice of a Daughter

I don't have the space to tell you what the Lord is doing in us through your book and videos. Another key came up from the first video when you spoke about older women mentoring the younger. We have a few older women who come to our meetings and they all said they got convicted about the need for this and how they wanted to do more and were seeking God on how.

–New Zealand

Do you hear their cry? They're not asking if we were perfect or even for us to be perfect now . . . they are asking for our help, for our wisdom. How can we turn away?

17. Explain the difference between forgiveness and consequences.

Big Idea

Truth breeds freedom as surely as shame perpetuates lies.

18. Does forgiveness eliminate consequences?

19. What does the Bible say about this?

20. Do you have any friends who you know have experienced God's forgiveness, yet the consequences seem to remain?

> ## Big Idea
>
> *On earth, forgiveness deals with sin and transgression, not necessarily consequences.*

21. How about you? Are there areas where you have suffered consequences even though you know you are forgiven?

Of course ultimately the day will come when and where none of us get what we really deserve. We all deserve judgment, and yet find mercy. God explained that on the earth it is a bit different.

> *"As long as the earth endures, seedtime and harvest, cold and heat, summer and winter, day and night will never cease." (Gen. 8:22)*

Voice of a Mother

A lot of what Kissed the Girls *said hit me in a very emotional way. I've done some fairly asinine things I'm scared of sharing with others, but it's something that I want to do. I want girls and young women to know it is okay to have their struggles and that someone is there for them. I never really understood some of the things I did were totally wrong. I had the mentality I had to do what the other person wanted me to do in order for him to like me. I've had a rough time understanding how God could forgive me for some of things I've done.*

–U.S.A.

Choices produce consequences. These are like seeds that spring up bringing good fruit forth as well as bad. When a seed is planted, is the plant immediately apparent? Of course not! The seed grows in secret before it sprouts and breaks the surface of the earth. At first, one seedling looks very much like another. What it will be or produce is not immediately apparent to the untrained eye.

Godly sorrow brings repentance that leads to salvation and leaves no regret, but worldly sorrow brings death. (2 Cor. 7:10)

Regret is removed when we confront any hardness of heart and our sorrow is no longer worldly, but godly in nature.

22. Define *godly sorrow:*

23. Who is an example of this in the Bible?

24. Define *worldly sorrow:*

25. Who is an example of this in the Bible?

> # Big Idea
>
> *When we openly own things, we are openly cleansed.*

26. Review Psalm 51, verses 10–13. What are the seven things God promises to accomplish in us in these verses?

-
-
-
-
-
-
-

27. What is an area in your life from which you could now teach transgressors His ways? A formally painful place which is now both healed and powerful?

Note to Moms

Write a letter to your daughter. It could be titled, "What I've Learned" or "What Life Has Taught Me." Every young girl would treasure such a gift from her mother. She would love to see you'd taken the time to do this out of foresight and love. You could keep these in a treasure box, and as need or season arose take them out and transfer them into your daughter's keeping. You could even have a treasure chest set up for her as well. These could be blessings as well as lessons from places of regret. They don't have to be long or perfect, just warm, honest, and composed as the Holy Spirit leads.

THE REGRET OF ABORTION . . . WHY IT'S NEVER A GOOD OPTION

There are six things the LORD hates, seven that are detestable to him: haughty eyes, a lying tongue, hands that shed innocent blood. (Prov. 6:16–17)

Is there any more innocent blood than that of an unborn child?

Let's lay aside all the arguments . . . what does God say about life in a womb? Listen to these beautiful and poetic words:

> *For you created my inmost being;*
> *you knit me together in my mother's womb.*
> *I praise you because I am fearfully and wonderfully made;*
> *your works are wonderful, I know that full well.*
> *My frame was not hidden from you when I was made in the secret place.*
> *When I was woven together in the depths of the earth, your eyes saw my unformed body.*
> *All the days ordained for me were written in your book before one of them came to be.*
> *How precious to me are your thoughts, O God!*
> *How vast is the sum of them! (Ps. 139:13–17)*

He writes our story before anyone sees our faces! First the spirit, or our inmost being, is created, and then our body is knit together in the still and safety of our mother's womb. While this is happening our heavenly Father lovingly records our days in His book. Perhaps He smiles as He makes notation of His thoughts toward us.

If you have experienced the pain of abortion, I need to speak healing to you. You may have been a frightened daughter who believed a lie.

You may have been the victim of violence.

Or perhaps it reached further . . . you are the mother who lost a grandchild.

Abortions are often not mourned openly. The beauty of a little life was swept neatly and efficiently away. Only afterward does the shroud of guilt and shame spread itself over the mother, the father, grandparents, and future sisters and brothers.

We live in a culture that is overwhelming selfish. It can never empower you to live in godliness, because it is governed by the fearful demands of self.

Most young girls who have gone to seek abortions have been counseled with this world's attractive reasons.

"You're young and beautiful . . . your whole life is ahead of you."

"Someday you will make a wonderful mother, but it is not your time now."

"The procedure is a matter of sloughing off cells, and you can return to your life and have children when you are ready."

"This baby is not wanted, and every child deserves to be wanted."

I know this because I have counseled and heard from women young and old who listened to this type of reasoning and ultimately relayed their regret.

I've been told they went into the clinic two people and came out a fractured, broken half.

The actual word *abortion* is not found in the Holy Scriptures as we know them, but it is referenced in the book of Enoch. He spoke of fallen angels and their instruction of the "striking of the embryo in the womb to diminish it." Other than this reference, there seems to be silence on the specific terminology. But what does God, the ultimate giver of life, say about unborn infants?

"Before I formed you in the womb I knew you." (Jer. 1:5)

28. Who is the One intimately involved with their formation?

Not only is He forming infants in the womb . . . He knows us then. While we grow in secret He lays out the days of our lives and stretches the path of destiny before us. Babies are not merely cells . . . they're lives. Gifts and visions of heaven entrusted to our wombs of earth. No one who has witnessed the wonder of the miracle of human birth can imagine these freshly emerged lives as anything other than potential and unique beauty.

Before I even missed a period with my third son I felt his life quicken within me. I felt weak during a worship service, and I felt myself swoon, so I took my seat and heard, "You carry life within you . . . there grows a son." I sensed His presence in that instant. Before I'd left the service, a young man I didn't even know approached me and said, "My mother looked over at you and said you have a life growing within you." That is how intimately acquainted God is with the life He entrusts to us.

But what if you did not know this?

What if you believed the lie that this life was an intrusion on yours?

What then?

In the wise words of David, who lost a child by way of selfish sin:

"Can I bring him back again? I will go to him, but he will not return to me." (2 Sam. 12:23)

No matter how painful and real the regret may be, we can never go back and change what happened. Our hope is found in looking ahead. We cannot punish ourselves enough . . . we must embrace God's truth as well as His forgiveness.

To do this we must move beyond excuses, reasoning, or a victim mentality, and call things what they really are. Abortion means the death of a child, a dream, and a destiny.

Too often a woman finds out only after her abortion that it has left her barren or subject to miscarriages. We aren't told about the high percentage of repeat abortions as the women fall right back into promiscuity . . . in a desperate attempt to feel even temporarily whole. At times it goes even deeper. They punish themselves, no longer allowing themselves to be "good girls." They spiral out of control. Others subconsciously try to replace the life they swept away.

In colleges many young women think of abortion as a rite of passage, and perhaps it is. It is a passage into the realm where we disconnect from everything that makes us nurturing and feminine. To accomplish this, we must shut down our hearts, for we were never meant to walk this dark hall of death. Children of God were created for paths of light.

> *The path of the righteous is like the first gleam of dawn, shining ever brighter till the full light of day. But the way of the wicked is like deep darkness; they do not know what makes them stumble. (Prov. 4:18–19)*

Some of us have found ourselves on the wrong path. We stumble and don't know why. No matter the reasons, it is time for you to now leave behind this way of darkness. There is no need to remain on this road in order to punish yourself, or serve some type of penance. It is time to flee this place of pain. Let's pray.

> *Father,*
>
> *Forgive me. Only You are the giver of life. I was afraid, deceived and selfish. I believed a lie, and now its darkness shadows me. I confess the sin of murder; I took a life. Forgive me. I offer no excuses—just my broken body, soul, and spirit. Heal me that I might again carry life. I want the light of love and light to permeate every place of secret darkness. Jesus, I know You are the door, and I walk through into the kingdom of Light. I renounce the power and the realm of the kingdom of darkness and receive You as my ultimate and loving Lord. Heal my broken heart and make it tender as You fill it with Your Holy Spirit's counsel. I step out of this womb of darkness into Your glorious light, and I receive Your healing now.*
>
> *— Your daughter*

HOLY MOMENT

Place your hand on your womb and be still. Breathe in God's presence as you bask in His goodness. I believe God has told me there are those of you He will heal of barrenness. Even now as you linger before Him He will break the curse of miscarriage and heal the scars in the walls of your womb. Let Him sweep away your guilt and shame.

Voice of a Mom

I have had it on my heart to speak to young girls and women and let them know your past doesn't have to dictate your future. That God is waiting to heal His daughters, how much He loves them, and they can be clean. I also want to share with them the price you pay for awaking love before you are ready, whether it was willing or not. Thank you for being obedient to God's call. Our daughters need this.

–U.S.A.

MY PRAYER FOR YOU

May every place of pain become a place of beauty and freedom as you reach out beyond yourself and teach transgressors the Word that has been made flesh in your life. May your words reach deep into the lives of others, just as God's have reached out to you.

Fifteen

WHY WE LOSE
WHEN WE GIVE IN

Taking Back Our Power

*R*ead chapter fifteen in *Kissed the Girls and Made Them Cry.*

Voice of a Daughter

I truly am tired of losing . . . I want my clothing.

–U.S.A.

"The unfair, ugly fact about the mating dance is that so much of female sexual power depends upon withholding oneself. If anything, that is even truer in an age when all the other girls are available, too."

–Lisa Schiffren, 1997 essay in The *Women's Quarterly,* page 97

1. What do you think about this quote? Do you think it is accurate?

2. Is it truly unfair?

In light of original intent—one man, one woman, one heart—I believe it is not unreasonable or unfair. Originally the man laid down his life for the love of one woman. I often wonder if we've unwittingly robbed men of their motivation. Where is the chaste beauty for the knight to rescue? Why should he brave it all?

The truth is most of us have blown it, yet the Prince desperately and passionately loves and longs for us. He is willing to brave it all to make us His own. As women make this connection we'll find ourselves restored and the hope of men stirred. We then find what we need, something men cannot give us . . . the power.

While reading to my sons the other night I revisited a story which captures this sentiment. The following is from C. S. Lewis's classic, *The Magician's Nephew*:

> *"Son of Adam," said Aslan, "you have sown well. And you, Narnians, let it be your first care to guard this Tree, for it is your shield. The Witch of whom I told you has fled far away into the North of the world; she will live on there, growing stronger in dark Magic. But while that Tree flourishes she will never come down into Narnia. She dare not come within a hundred miles of the Tree, for its smell, which is joy and life and health to you, is death and horror and despair to her."*
>
> *". . . The Witch has already eaten one of those apples, one of the same kind that Tree grew from."*
>
> *. . . "So we thought Aslan," she said, "that there must be some mistake, and she can't really mind the smell of those apples."*
>
> *"Why do you think that, Daughter of Eve?" asked the Lion.*
>
> *"Well, she ate one."*
>
> *"Child," he replied, "that is why all the rest are now a horror to her. That is what happens to those who pluck and eat fruits at the wrong time and in the wrong way. The fruit is good, but they loathe it ever after."*
>
> *"Oh I see," said Polly. "And I suppose because she took it in the wrong way it won't work with her. I mean it won't make her young and all that?"*
>
> *"Alas," said Aslan, shaking his head. "It will. Things always work according to their nature. She has won her heart's desire; she has unwearying strength and endless days like a goddess. But length of days with an evil heart is only length of misery and already she begins to know it. All get what they want: they do not always like it."*
>
> *(pages 173–174)*

In this ageless story I see our sad, present position. We've plucked fruit at the wrong time and in the wrong way, and the joy has slipped away. Every voice of our culture cries "Take it, take it now!" But what is the cry of the daughters?

Voice of a Daughter

It's personally taken a lot for me to let go and allow Jesus to make me the woman He always created me to be, rather than the one created by my own upbringing, misconceptions, media, and just LIFE IN GENERAL. Jesus has been teaching me what He says a woman really is and it is so different from what the world tells us.

–New Zealand

In closing we will end where we began . . . it's all about the power.

> How can we live without the power?
> How can we love without the power?
> How can we long for Him without the power?
> How can we be lovely without the power?

We must choose to lay hold of truth! Because daughters, it's our time to win.

And where is this power to be found?
Only in Him.

3. What do you think of the current reality programs on TV?

4. Why do you think there is such a longing for "real"?

Voice of a Daughter

I recently finished Kissed the Girls, *and it is truly one of the most insightful books I've ever read. I appreciate your honesty. I wish I'd known when I was a teen it's not about "how close I can get to the line without crossing it"; but about "how pure and radiant can I be for my Bridegroom?" I am so thankful I know now!*

–U.S.A.

I often fear we long for real because in our desperate longing for truth we have substituted reality. We look around and find so much that is false. We hear so many lies that we decide to choose hard, cold reality rather than pursue the beauty of the dream.

I've heard this logic repeatedly: "The boys have used us, so now we use them."

Is anyone winning here? The men are not. The women are not. As far as I am concerned, if this is reality . . . I'll take the dream! As you look around, be careful to *never confuse reality with truth.*

5. What is the defining difference between *reality* and *truth*?

Promiscuity is costly for men, but not in comparison to the price it exacts from women.

6. List some reasons why this is true:

Big Idea

Women suffer the greatest when the laws of love are desecrated.

I believe this is a product of the Garden struggle. But we've left the Garden of transgression and stepped into His glorious light. We've closed the door and should no longer conduct ourselves as intimates of shame.

We are on the verge of restoration. I hear it in my spirit. The daughters are coming forth out of their pain and shame and walking again in light and beauty.

Voice of a Daughter

The majority of the time you want things His way and trust His plan—there are those times though when the temptation is there to rely on yourself and your "old tricks" to get what you want in case Jesus can't make it happen. I'm realizing very quickly how futile and damaging this is and that no matter how many times we do try this it's never going to work . . .

—New Zealand

---

7. How have you compromised your dream?

Big Idea

Women are at their strongest when they are women.

8. How have you allowed others to strip you of your position of respect and therefore authority?

9. It is time we stopped acting like men. What are the areas where you have abandoned your feminine side in your relationships?

If we want to recover our power and establish intimacy, we must be reconciled to truth. We must put back on our clothing so we will have something to reveal. Sexual liberation has degraded the image of women of all ages. You can have seduction without femininity, but femininity carries with it an allure of mystery.

HOLY MOMENT

Ask the Holy Spirit what areas of your life need to be covered and reconciled with the freedom and power available in truth.

The current problem: For centuries daughters of Eve have cried out to the sons of Adam, "Give me sacrificial love, rescue and protect me. Meet my deepest need for security and safety." When Adam answers, he makes declarations he cannot keep in the hope she will meet a yearning he cannot verbalize. Both are doomed to fail because God alone wants to meet these deep desires in us. Here on earth He gives the sons and daughters of Adam and Eve but a glimpse and a longing of the joy unspeakable to come.

It is not the fault of the sons of Adam; they cannot render to us the blessing we seek, and we have frightened them by giving them so much power over our souls. We must learn, as Jacob did, the blessings only come from God. We must allow God to give us a new name, for we are no longer wrestling daughters of Eve hiding in shadows but daughters of light and promise, His bride.

Song to Make It Real
Rooftops

I was lost
I was afraid until You found me
And You took me by the hand
I was bound
I was in chains
Until You came and set me free to dance again

Now I'm screaming at the top of my lungs

You are good I know
I will shout it from the rooftops
You are good I know
That Your love will go forever
You are good

I was blind but now I see
From the rooftops I will sing
I was bound but now I'm free

By Glenn Packiam and Jon Egan, from the Desperation Band album *From the Rooftops*

© 2004 Vertical Worship Songs/ASCAP

It is our time to dance, daughters; embrace all He has for you!

Voice of a Daughter

Reading your book I found a place where I felt known on the inside. A journey took place that allowed the most beautiful polishing of a work He had already begun. As I read through each page I screamed, "YES!! YES!!" as I discovered Truth and the model of "woman" in a way that's very close to my own heart. I began to find my innocence again and the type of rest that comes from being the daughter of a Father who actually protects her and keeps her. Not for His own appetite but to release her into the good plan He has for her life. I have also been reading the book of Esther, which was a beautiful parallel to reading Kissed the Girls. *There has been such a hunger in my heart to be a "woman" of God. And to see more of them stand and lead this generation into a revelation of what it is to be one! God has brought a great end to 25 years of restlessness. I am grateful for the anointing to break the yoke!*

—Australia

This about says it all. In this great story of life there is a role only you can fill. It is not the one the dark prince cast you in. In this role there is no shame, judgment, rejection, or fear—there is only beauty, love, and of course splendor. Leave behind the shadow world and step onto this new stage and place for your life. I will close with this promise and prayer. As Paul passed this letter to the church at Ephesus, I now pass this letter on to you, my daughter, my sister, my mother, for the whole world holds its breath awaiting your appearance. Allow it to enfold you in its love:

Voice of a Daughter

There is no other way. He truly does make something precious and beautiful out of something that was so screwed up and desperate. I never loved being one of Jesus' girls more than I do now and am so proud and thankful of the work He has done. Only He and I know what I was really like before He got a hold of me—as does every other precious sister He's rescued.

—New Zealand

Dearest Daughters of the Most High,

I have not stopped giving thanks for you, remembering you in my prayers. I keep asking that the God of our Lord Jesus Christ, the glorious Father, may give you the Spirit of wisdom and revelation, so that you may know Him better.

I pray also that the eyes of your heart may be enlightened in order that you may know the hope to which He has called you, the riches of His glorious inheritance in the saints, and His incomparably great power for us who believe.

That power is like the working of His mighty strength, which He exerted in Christ when He raised Him from the dead and seated Him at His right hand in the heavenly realms, far above all rule and authority, power and dominion, and every title that can be given, not only in the present age but also in the one to come.

And God placed all things under His feet and appointed Him to be head over everything for the church, which is His body, the fullness of Him who fills everything in every way.

As for you, you were dead in your transgressions and sins, in which you used to live when you followed the ways of this world and of the ruler of the kingdom of the air, the spirit who is now at work in those who are disobedient.

All of us also lived among them at one time, gratifying the cravings of our sinful nature and following its desires and thoughts. Like the rest, we were by nature objects of wrath. But because of His great love for us, God, who is rich in mercy, made us alive with Christ even when we were dead in transgressions—it is by grace you have been saved.

And God raised us up with Christ and seated us with Him in the heavenly realms in Christ Jesus, in order that in the coming ages He might show the incomparable riches of His grace, expressed in His kindness to us in Christ Jesus. For it is by grace you have been saved, through faith—and this not from yourselves, it is the gift of God—not by works, so that no one can boast. For we are God's workmanship, created in Christ Jesus to do good works, which God prepared in advance for us to do.   (Ephesians 1:16–2:10)

May our faithful loving Father watch over His glorious promises to perform them in your precious lives. Take all He has for you and don't draw back, daughters of the Most High.

> *In His love,*
>
> *Lisa*

ANSWER KEY

CHAPTER 2

Question # 7: The woman was stripped of the noble origin of women and her authority as completion and helpmeet of man. She exchanged joint and complementary dominion for grasping and manipulation. The man was reduced to a position of domination and blaming as he laid aside his role as the strong, protective male provider.

Question # 11: Men cannot complete other men, just as women can never find their completion in other women.

Question # 18: The serpent's goal has always been the same . . . to strip the daughters of Eve of their dignity, strength, and honor.

Question # 19: When women are stripped, the men are shamed as well, for the woman is the glory of the man (1 Cor. 11:7).

Question # 23: You need to be outraged. For only then you will find the courage to fight your true enemy and give your allegiance to the faithful and true King. You cry out for the love of a heavenly Prince. And I have a secret to tell you whether you believe it or not . . . He longs desperately for you as well.

CHAPTER 3

Question # 2: The Scriptures tell us they were literally looking for a way to trap Jesus in order to arrest Him. The woman was just a pawn.

Question # 8: Under the law, men were to be held equally responsible for their actions. Sexual promiscuity and perversion is an affront to God's original plan of one man, one woman, with one heart. The relationship between man and woman was always to be symbolic of Christ and the Church.

Question # 12: "Jesus Christ is the same yesterday and today and forever" (Heb. 13:8).

Question # 18: He entices us into captivity by way of rebellion and then imprisons us with the lie of no escape.

CHAPTER 4

Question # 2: Time and energy

Question # 3: Priorities

Question # 4: They will be years of strength and empowering relationships rather than a season of folly and foolishness. The friendships you develop around the pursuit of God will be a source of joy and strength, rather than a dynamic of shame or embarrassment.

Question # 9: It is a season of preparation, like soldiers in boot camp.

Question # 10:

- He first loves us. (1 John 4:19)
- His love will not change.

Question # 11: In the same manner we'd awaken natural romantic love, but with a different focus.

Question # 26: By words and actions

CHAPTER 7

Question # 19: It means "to run from in terror."

CHAPTER 12

Question # 5: *Holiness* means set apart or consecrated while *purity* is the manner in which we conduct ourselves because we *are* set apart. *Holiness* declares who we belong to, and *purity* is the effect of being separated.

CHAPTER 14

Question # 6: We attempt to avoid consequences by learning to be sneaky.

Question # 7: As adults we're rarely policed in our motives or actions and therefore rarely have to answer to immediate consequences (unless by an employer or submitting to an accountability group). If we are not careful, as we age we'll hone our skills of justifying rather than hiding our actions.

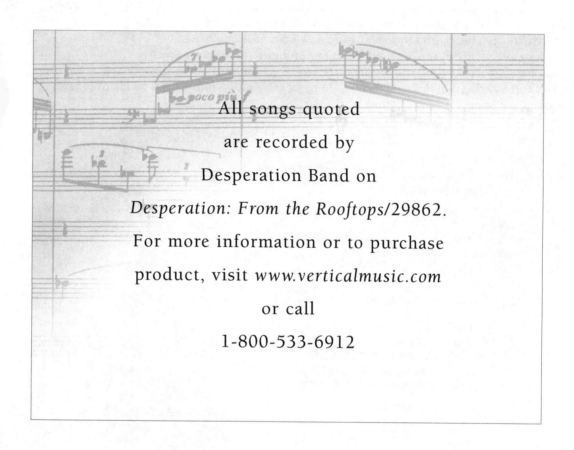

All songs quoted
are recorded by
Desperation Band on
Desperation: From the Rooftops/29862.
For more information or to purchase
product, visit *www.verticalmusic.com*
or call
1-800-533-6912

Contact us today to receive your free copy of Messenger International's newsletter and our 24 page color catalog of ministry resources!

The vision of MI is to strengthen believers, awaken the lost and captive in the church and proclaim the knowledge of His glory to the nations. John and Lisa are reaching millions of people each year through television and by ministering at churches, bible schools and conferences around the world. We long to see God's Word in the hands of leaders and hungry believers in every part of the earth.

MESSENGER INTERNATIONAL
w w w . l i s a b e v e r e . o r g
with John and Lisa Bevere

UNITED STATES
PO Box 888
Palmer Lake, CO 80133-0888
800-648-1477 (US & Canada)
Tel: 719-487-3000
Fax: 719-487-3300
E-mail: jbm@johnbevere.org

EUROPE
PO Box 622
Newport, NP19 8ZJ
UNITED KINGDOM
Tel: 44 (0) 870-745-5790
Fax: 44 (0) 870-745-5791
E-mail: jbmeurope@johnbevere.org

AUSTRALIA
PO Box 6200
Dural, D.C. NSW 2158
Australia
In AUS 1-300-650-577
Tel: +61 2 8850 1725
Fax +61 2 8850 1735
Email: jbmaustralia@johnbevere.org

Lisa is the bestselling author of *Kissed the Girls and Made Them Cry*, *Out of Control ar Loving It*, *Be Angry But Don't Blow It!* and more. In addition to national and internation conferences, Lisa is a frequent guest on television shows like *Life Today* and radio programs suc as **Focus of the Family** and **Family Life Today**. She co-hosts the weekly television program "Th Messenger" which broadcasts to 214 nations. Lisa's style is real and transparent bringing freedom to women of all ages, challenging them to face their fears and embrace fearless living. Lisa anc her husband John, also a bestselling author make their home in Colorado with their four sons.

KISSED THE GIRLS AND MADE THEM CRY
CURRICULUM

Lisa's Debut Curriculum

Included on the DVD...

Session One	How Far is Too Far?
Session Two	Packaging is Power
Session Three	Restoring the Dream
Session Four	Purity's Promise

5 VHS Series included in this Kit

Includes over an hour of never before seen Bonus **Q&A**

- 5 VHS TAPES
- 4 DVDs (INCLUDES BONUS Q&A SESSION)
- 4 AUDIO CDs OF THE VIDEO SESSIONS
- 1 MUSIC CD
- KISSED THE GIRLS AND MADE THEM CRY BOOK
- STUDENT WORKBOOK • 2 POSTERS

We are presently in a sexual nightmare, but God longs to give us a dream. Purity's Power is a call for women to live in the freedom and confidence of God's love, looking to no one but Him for their strength and security. This series is not a list of rules for girls to follow or a prescription for purity. Rather, it is a guide to help women of all ages understand how their relationship with God affects the sexual aspect of their lives. Using scripture, Lisa explains how femininity empowers women to live in freedom.

What one mother said!   TESTIMONY

All by "chance" I became the thrilled and proud owner of your series. After working and crying through the series and book with a friend both of us seeking knowledge for the sake of our daughters, 8 & 7, and healing from our youthful choices, we both blurted out, almost simultaneously, "The youth need to see this!"

I can hardly believe what God has done! I have gone from a woman who: didn't like being a teen, didn't like teenagers, never wanted to work with them. (They scared me!) And I certainly DID NOT want to talk about sex with them. To a woman who can't wait to gather these young sisters and share these messages with them.

Thank you, Lisa, for an awesome teaching that has brought me healing and will bring many young women the tools to be all God has intended them to be.

CBA Best-Selling Book

Kissed The Girls And Made Them Cry
Why women lose when they give in

Women are admitting promiscuity isn't really getting them what they wanted after all - because as women we always stand to lose so much more than men when we give in. We were created for so much more than a sexual outlet for men, and as women, we want and deserve more than just sexual release for ourselves. It is time to restore dignity, honor, strength - and yes, even power to generations of women, young and old, who are no longer willing to lose. This book answers some hard-hitting questions with God empowered open and frank answers.

To incorporate this life changing series, contact us at *www.lisabevere.org* or call us at *Messenger International* **1-800-648-1477**. You will find additional information in the back of this workbook.

---

ll songs quoted are recorded by Desperation Band on "Desperation: From the Rooftops"/29862. For more information or to purchase oduct, visit verticalmusic.com or call 1-800-533-6912

FEATURED MESSAGES FROM LISA

Seizing Your Moment - VHS

There are issues in life where timing is not just important...*it is everything!* The Word declares, *"Now Faith Is!"* God is always in the moment. By living in the moment we increase our awareness of where we are in the dimension of time. With this understanding comes the ability to eat the fruit of our season. You may be in the season of youth, middle age, or the wisdom of golden years, but no matter what your season, *it is time for the generations of women to connect!*

How do you know if it is your moment? Often there is a quickening or excitement. If we respond there is life, if not we have to wait for the next wave. But if you seize your moment...you will get what you need to move forward...*something powerful called momentum!*

Healing For The Angry Heart - *4 VHS, 4 Audio CD or 7 Cassette series*

How does one successfully manage negative emotions, which can damage personal relationships or even prove self-destructive? The roots of anger can be found deep within the hearts of men, women and even children. However, *before hearts can be healed and anger problems resolved, inner conflicts must be recognized and emotional issues must be addressed.* Lisa discusses: Her testimony of healing, the power of confession and stopping anger before it gets out of hand.

Life Without Limits - DVD or VHS

Our life is not our own, so why not take off the limits? Eph 3:20 promises, *"Now to him who is able to do immeasurably more than all we ask or imagine, according to his power that is at work within us, (NIV)* it is definitely no longer about us, but it is about Him! God is calling to a generation of women who will take the risks and go out where it is over their heads. Women who will be brave enough to trust Him with every area of their lives. He is watching for wild women who will be reckless in both their abandonment to God and their commitment to obedience. It is time to embrace His freedom in every area of our lives.

It's Time - Audio CD

IT'S NOT YOUR TURN...IT'S YOUR TIME!
For too long we have had the attitude, "It's my turn!" But when God begins to pour out His spirit, it is nobody's turn, it becomes everybody's time. It's time for God's gifts in His body to come forth.
The Father is gifting men and women alike to shine in each and every realm of life. Discover what He has placed in your hand and join the dance of a lifetime.
You have saved the best 'til now. ~ John 2:10 (NIV)

Books by John

* A Heart Ablaze
* The Bait of Satan
* Breaking Intimidation
* The Devil's Door
* Drawing Near

* ❖ The Fear of the Lord
* ❖ Thus Saith the Lord?
* ❖ Under Cover
* ❖ Victory in the Wilderness
* ❖ The Voice of One Crying

ALSO...

ORDER JOHN'S LATEST CURRICULUM TODAY!

HARD COVER BOOK • LEADERS GUIDE
STUDENT WORKBOOK • 5 VHS TAPES • 4 DVDs
6 AUDIO CDs • A PROMO KIT • 2 POSTERS

PLEASE VISIT *www.lisabevere.org*
CALL US FOR MORE INFORMATION: 1-800-648-1477 (US & CANADA)
Australia: +61 2 8850 1725 • *Europe:* 44 (0) 870-745-5790